The Ultimate Ice Cre

ON-LINE

Also by Bruce Weinstein

Frozen Drinks With or Without the Buzz

The Ultimate

Ice Cream Book

OVER 500 ICE CREAMS, SORBETS, GRANITAS, DRINKS, AND MORE

BRUCE WEINSTEIN

WILLIAM MORROW AND COMPANY, INC. · NEW YORK

It is the policy of William Morrow and Company, Inc., and its
imprints and affiliates, recognizing the importance of
preserving what has been written, to print the books we
publish on acid-free paper, and we exert our best efforts
to that end.

Library of Congress Cataloging-in-Publication Data

Weinstein, Bruce, 1960-
     The ultimate ice cream book : over 500 ice creams, sorbets,
granitas, drinks, and more / Bruce Weinstein. —1st ed.
       p. cm.
     Includes index.
     ISBN 0-688-16149-9
     1. Ice cream, ices, etc. [. Title.
     TX795 .W45 1999
     641.8'62—dc21

                                                    98–45352
                                                    CIP

Printed in the United States of America

First Edition

1   2   3   4   5   6   7   8   9   10

BOOK DESIGN BY JO ANNE METSCH

www.williammorrow.com

To Mark Scarbrough,

the kindest and most generous man I know.

His taste and inspiration fill my life

as well as every recipe in this book.

ACKNOWLEDGMENTS

Heartfelt thanks to Susan Ginsburg, my agent, for her perseverance and encouragement, and to John Hodgeman at Writers House for keeping everything flowing;

At William Morrow, Justin Schwartz, editor and food maven, for having the vision to create this book and for making the whole process so easy, and Christy Stabin for getting my ducks in a row;

Rick Rodgers, my friend and colleague, for his support and advice right from the start;

Julie Weinstein, David Sisson, Debbie Weinstein, Dan Rome, Carol Altes, Alethea Worden, Alex Laird, and Danny Feinman, who ate their way through my freezer without ever looking back;

Esther Lou Scarbrough, for sharing old family recipes and sending pistachios and pecans all the way from Texas.

I would also like to gratefully acknowledge Williams-Sonoma.

CONTENTS

INTRODUCTION

When I started putting together recipes for this book, I wanted to re-create ice creams with the flavors and textures found in an old-fashioned ice cream parlor—a place where classic ice creams and traditional toppings held court. There, handwritten blackboards announced what was made each day, and toppings such as hot fudge, marshmallow, and butterscotch were commonplace. Lemongrass-ginger sauces and cassis-cabernet reductions were simply not on the menu.

But I also wanted to create flavors for today's more adventurous palates—refreshing flavor combinations that could satisfy even the most sophisticated among us. So I've put together a collection of classic ice cream flavors, and then customized them with mix-ins and simple substitutions. Each basic recipe is followed by a list of variations designed to push the idea just a little, and then some more. You should even feel free to write your own variations in the margins. After all, you can have your ice cream and eat it, too.

ABOUT THE RECIPES

THERE are two basic styles of ice cream in this book: custard-style ice cream (sometimes called "frozen custard," "French ice cream," or "gelato"), which is made with eggs; and Philadelphia-style ice cream, which is made without eggs. In tasting after tasting, I found the custard-style ice creams richer than their Philadelphia-style counterparts. The Philadelphia-style ice creams, however, are much easier to make.

Re-creating the authentic custard-style ice cream of those old-fashioned ice cream emporia means using plenty of eggs—a potential problem if the eggs are not properly cooked. Certainly, not all eggs contain harmful bacteria; nonetheless, it is possible to get ill from eating contaminated raw eggs. So I created recipes that call only for *cooked* eggs, that is, heated to a safe temperature before chilling and freezing the ice cream mixture.

Traditionally, sorbets are made with fruit, sugar, and water, while sherbets also contain egg whites or possibly milk. Today, on the other hand, most ices are called sorbets as long as they don't contain heavy cream. Indeed, I opt for a simpler, perhaps clearer distinction: ice cream vs. sorbet. Despite the fact that some would call these sherbets, I have created a few sorbets that contain egg whites and/or skim milk. In keeping with my desire for safety, all egg whites are "cooked" by beating in a hot sugar syrup.

Eggs present a second problem as well: how to divide them when reducing a recipe. The easiest way is to beat the total number of eggs called for in the recipe and then measure the volume. You can then use the amount you need, whether it's half the volume or a third or a quarter. Cover and store any remaining eggs in the refrigerator for tomorrow's scrambled eggs.

Fruit is the main flavoring for most of the ice creams and sorbets in this book. Canned or frozen fruits are acceptable for many but not all of the recipes. Canned peaches, for instance, do not have enough flavor to cut through the cream and sugar. Canned purple plums, on the other hand, make a wonderfully full-flavored ice cream. In fact, sometimes I recommend canned fruit over fresh. For example, fresh pineapple contains an enzyme that breaks down the protein in the milk, causing it to curdle. When pineapple is canned, this enzyme is destroyed, making the fruit usable in ice cream. So how do you know when to use canned, frozen, or fresh fruit? Unless otherwise specified, use fresh fruit. The recipes tell you whether canned or frozen fruit is an acceptable substitute.

Fresh fruit for ice cream should be ripe, sweet, and juicy. Taste it (if you can) before you buy it, but by all means smell it. After all, our sense of smell accounts for much of our tasting ability. Most fruits, including peaches, plums, cherries, apples, pears, mangoes, and pineapples, smell sweet and fragrant when ripe. When using canned or frozen fruit, always look for premium quality. Select canned fruit packed in juice, not heavy syrup (unless otherwise called for). Frozen fruit should be packed without syrup or sauce.

I don't recommend using artificial flavorings and extracts in most of these ice creams, but there is one exception: the only way to make good bubble gum ice cream is with artificial bubble gum flavoring. But for vanilla or almond flavor, the real thing is always best. A few years back I discovered double-strength vanilla from Penzeys in Muskego, Wisconsin (414-574-0277), and have sworn by it ever since. They also carry premium-quality spices and lavender flowers, which are called for in some of the recipes in this book.

ICE CREAM MACHINES

AN ice cream machine is essential for making good ice creams and sorbets. The machine churns the mixture as it freezes, incorporating air in the process. The result is smooth and creamy, avoiding the Popsicle syndrome—a solid block of cream and ice that's impossible to serve or eat. Yes, I have also seen ice cream made by stirring liquid nitrogen into sweetened, flavored heavy cream. But unless you are a research chemist and like to cook wearing thick asbestos gloves, I don't recommend this technique. In the end, there's no way around it. Unless you want to sit in a walk-in freezer, stirring a bowl of cream and fruit, you need to get a machine. Fortunately, you have a wide choice, ranging in both price and style.

The machines with built-in compressors are easiest to use. They churn and freeze at the touch of a button. These machines work fast, incorporating minimal air into the mixture, thereby turning out a dense, premium ice cream. You can also make as many batches of ice cream as you like, one right after the other. The only drawback is their hefty price tag. Plan to spend anywhere from $300 to $600.

Ice cream makers with canisters you chill in the freezer before use are also easy, and not nearly as expensive. When you're ready to make ice cream, remove the canister from the freezer, insert it into your machine, pour in the ice cream or sorbet mixture, and flip the switch or crank away. The electric type is obviously easier, but both make rich, dense ice cream. There's only one drawback: you can make only one batch of ice cream before having to refreeze the canister, sometimes overnight. One-quart models with motors cost around $50; the equivalent hand-crank model is about $25. If you plan to make a lot of ice cream, buy two or three of these machines so you can churn multiple batches without interruption.

Ice cream makers that require ice and rock salt take longer to freeze the ice cream or sorbet, thereby incorporating more air into the mixture and producing a lighter, airier dessert. Personally I prefer the dense, rich quality of ice creams and sorbets made quickly. It's all a matter of taste, and if you want an old-fashioned ice cream maker, you can easily find hand-cranked and motorized versions. Plan to spend over $150 for a wooden model or substantially less for a plastic version.

All three types of ice cream machines do a good job of making the recipes in this book. Keep in mind that the easier the machine is to use, the more likely you are to use it. Every recipe in this book can be doubled or tripled, should you choose a large-capacity ice cream maker. Ice cream custard will keep in the refrigerator for up to two days, so multiplying a recipe allows you make fresh ice cream every day, without starting from scratch.

MIX-INS

MANY of the ice cream variations in this book call for the addition of cookies, crackers, wafers, biscotti, or cake. These ice creams are best served as soon as they're made, while the mix-ins are still crunchy. One way to ensure a longer "crunch" life is to first let the mix-in ingredients dry out overnight. This will keep them from becoming soggy before the ice cream can freeze around them. Setting the crumbled cake, cookies, crackers, or biscotti in a 300°F degree oven for five to ten minutes can also help ensure a crunchy mix-in. Take care not to overbake them, and remember to let them cool completely before mixing them into the chilled ice cream.

To toast nuts and coconut for ice cream mix-ins or toppings, preheat the oven to 400°F degrees. Spread the nuts or coconut in a thin layer on a baking sheet or aluminum foil. Bake for 5 to 10 minutes, then remove from the oven when the nuts are fragrant and just beginning to brown, or when the coconut is light golden brown. Take care to check often, so as not to burn the nuts or coconut. Allow them to cool before using.

Many variations also require you to "swirl" jam or sauce into the finished ice cream. To swirl properly, wait until the machine has finished freezing the ice cream or sorbet. Then remove the dasher or mixer before spooning the jam or sauce over the soft frozen ice cream. Lightly swirl in a zigzag pattern with a small knife or a fork. An alternate way to achieve a simple swirl is to "layer" it. To do this, remove one third of the finished ice cream or sorbet from the machine and spoon it into a freezer-safe container. Cover it with one third of the jam or sauce. Repeat, making layers with the remaining ice cream and jam or sauce. Place the layered ice cream or sorbet in the freezer to firm it up before serving.

TIPS ON DRINKS

MORE than any other ingredient, ice cubes have the greatest influence on frozen drinks, shakes, and malts. For best results, let your ice cubes sit at room temperature for fifteen minutes before using; this softens the ice and results in creamier drinks. Smaller ice cubes also blend in easier for thick and creamy drinks. To make smaller cubes, simply fill your ice cube trays halfway.

It's no surprise that ice cream has become a staple of birthday parties, anniversaries, and holidays throughout the year. Ice cream is not the means to a celebration; ice cream is a celebration in itself. And whether you've been making your own ice cream for years or are about to crank your very first machine, this book can guide you through hundreds of ways to celebrate a glorious dessert.

Ice Cream Cones

. . . .

If you're going to the trouble to make your own ice cream, why not spend a few more minutes and make your own cones? Here are three simple, delicious ways to make this time-honored ice cream vehicle. The cones are fun, easy, and better than store-bought. Use these basic recipes and the nine variations as a start, then be creative. After your cones have cooled, dip them in melted chocolate, then into nuts, sprinkles, or chopped candy.

OVEN-BAKED SUGAR CONES

THESE cones taste somewhat like fortune cookies and are very sturdy. They're easiest to make if you have a nonstick cookie sheet and cone-shaped molds, which are available at baking supply stores or by mail from Bridge Kitchenware in New York City (212-688-4220).

¾ cup sugar

1 large egg

2 tablespoons butter, melted and cooled

1 teaspoon vanilla extract

¼ cup milk

½ cup all-purpose flour, sifted

Preheat the oven to 300°F. In a medium mixing bowl, beat the sugar into the egg until it is thickened and pale yellow. Beat in the butter, vanilla, and milk. Gently stir in the flour.

Grease a large nonstick cookie sheet and spread 1½ tablespoons of the batter into a 6-inch circle using a thin, flexible spatula. Dipping the spatula in water first makes this job easier. The batter will spread about ½ inch while baking, so keep the circles about 1 inch apart. Fit as many circles as you can on 1 cookie sheet.

Bake for 15 minutes or until lightly browned. Remove the cookie sheet from the oven and use a large metal spatula to remove 1 cookie from the sheet. Handling it carefully so as not to burn your hands, immediately wrap the hot, pliable cookie around a cone-shaped mold, sealing the point. Repeat with the remaining cookies. The cookies will harden as they cool, so work as quickly as possible. Let the cookie sheet cool and repeat the process with the remaining batter. Remove the cones from the molds when completely cool.

◂ • ▸

Variations

BOWL CONES Invert 4 small, clean, identical bowls to use as molds. Place hot cookies directly over the bottoms of the bowls. The cookies will fall around the sides of the bowls and harden as they cool. When cool enough to handle, carefully remove the cones from the bowls and repeat with any remaining warm cookies.

continued

ITALIAN CONES Add a few drops of anise extract or ¼ teaspoon ground fennel to the batter along with the vanilla. Proceed with the recipe as directed.

WALNUT CONES Stir ⅓ cup finely chopped walnuts into the finished batter. Proceed with the recipe as directed.

> *Hint: If your cones aren't quite perfect (OK, so there's a hole on the bottom), don't worry. Carefully stuff the bottom with a few mini-marshmallows to keep the ice cream from leaking out as it melts.*

PIZELLE WAFFLE CONES

THESE cones require a pizelle iron—a round waffle iron with very shallow grooves. Electric and stovetop models are available. Look for them at baking supply stores or by mail from Bridge Kitchenware in New York City (212-688-4220).

¼ cup sugar

1 large egg

5 tablespoons butter, melted and cooled

1 teaspoon vanilla extract

⅓ cup all-purpose flour, sifted

In a medium mixing bowl, beat the sugar into the egg until it is thickened and pale yellow. Beat in the butter and vanilla. Gently stir in the flour. Do not overmix or the pizelle may become tough. Allow the batter to rest at room temperature at least 15 minutes.

Lightly grease your pizelle iron with vegetable oil spray. Preheat the iron on the stove over medium heat (if you're using an electric model, follow the manufacturer's directions). Use 1½ tablespoons of batter for a 5-inch pizelle iron and 2 tablespoons for an 8-inch pizelle iron. Close the iron and cook the pizelle for 30 seconds on one side. Turn the iron over and continue to cook until lightly golden, about 1 minute more. Carefully peel the soft cookie off the iron and roll it around a cone-shaped mold, sealing the point. Repeat with remaining batter. The cones will harden as they cool. Remove the cones from the molds when completely cool.

◄ • ►

Variations

ALMOND CONES Substitute ¼ teaspoon almond extract for the vanilla extract. Proceed with the recipe as directed.

CINNAMON CONES Add ½ teaspoon ground cinnamon to the batter along with the vanilla. Proceed with the recipe as directed.

CIRCUS CONES Add a few drops of food coloring to the batter along with the vanilla. Proceed with the recipe as directed.

FLOWER CONES Add 1 teaspoon rose water or orange flower water to the batter along with the vanilla. Proceed with the recipe as directed.

MERINGUE CONES

THESE aren't true cones; in fact, they're not even shaped like cones—more like shells. They're still a great way to serve ice cream. And since so many recipes call for egg yolks, I found these meringues a great way to use up all those leftover egg whites.

4 large egg whites

⅛ teaspoon salt

⅛ teaspoon cream of tartar

1 cup superfine sugar

Preheat the oven to 180°F. In a large mixing bowl, beat the egg whites with an electric mixer on medium speed until foamy. Add the salt and cream of tartar. Continue to beat until soft peaks form. Slowly beat in the sugar, turn the beater to high, and continue to beat until the mixture is thick and shiny, about 2 minutes.

Butter and flour a large cookie sheet. Create the shells by placing ½ cup of meringue, in a mound, on the cookie sheet. Using a wet spoon, make a depression in the center about 4 inches wide (big enough to hold a large scoop of ice cream). Take care to leave at least ¼ inch of meringue on the bottom.

The meringue shells will not spread, so place them close together and fit as many as you can on the cookie sheet. Bake for 2 hours. Turn off the oven and open its door. Allow the meringues to sit in the oven until cool. Store in an airtight container until ready to use.

‹ • ›

Variations

CHOCOLATE CHIP MERINGUES Mix ¾ cup miniature chocolate chips into the meringue just before creating mounds. Proceed with the recipe as directed.

CINNAMON MERINGUES Add ½ teaspoon ground cinnamon along with the sugar. Proceed with the recipe as directed.

Ice Creams

ALMOND ICE CREAM

ALMOND paste, sometimes called marzipan, can be found in the baking aisle of most supermarkets or from New York Cake and Baking Distributors (800-942-2539). The most common package is a 7- or 8-ounce tube or can.

7 ounces almond paste

⅔ cup sugar

3 large eggs

½ teaspoon almond extract

¼ teaspoon salt

2 cups half-and-half

1 cup heavy cream

Combine the almond paste and sugar in a medium bowl and beat with an electric mixer until the mixture is completely smooth. Add the eggs one at a time, beating well after each addition. Beat in the almond extract and salt.

Bring the half-and-half to a simmer in a heavy medium saucepan. Slowly beat the hot half-and-half into the almond paste mixture. Pour the entire mixture back into the pan and place over low heat. Stir constantly with a whisk or wooden spoon until the custard thickens slightly. Be careful not to let the mixture boil or the eggs will scramble. Remove from the heat and pour the hot almond custard through a strainer into a large, clean bowl. Allow the custard to cool slightly, then stir in the heavy cream. Cover and refrigerate until cold or overnight.

Stir the chilled custard, then freeze in 1 or 2 batches in your ice cream machine according to the manufacturer's instructions. When finished, the ice cream will be soft but ready to eat. For firmer ice cream, transfer to a freezer-safe container and freeze at least 2 hours.

Variations

ALMOND LINZERTORTE ICE CREAM Stir 2 tablespoons water into ½ cup raspberry jam to loosen it up. Swirl the jam plus 2 tablespoons chopped toasted almonds (see page xvi) into the finished ice cream. Take care not to overswirl or the jam will "melt" into the ice cream. Streaks of jam should be visible. Serve immediately or freeze until firm.

ALMOND POPPY SEED ICE CREAM Add 2 teaspoons poppy seeds to the custard along with the cream. Proceed with the recipe as directed.

continued

CHOCOLATE ALMOND ICE CREAM Add 4 ounces chopped semisweet chocolate to the half-and-half before simmering. Stir until the mixture simmers and the chocolate is completely melted. Proceed with the recipe as directed.

ITALIAN ALMOND ICE CREAM Add ¼ cup amaretto liqueur to the custard before freezing. Add ½ cup crumbled amaretti cookies to the machine when the ice cream is semi-frozen. Allow the machine to mix in the cookies. Proceed with the recipe as directed.

STRAWBERRY ALMOND ICE CREAM Stir 2 tablespoons water into ½ cup strawberry preserves to loosen it up. Swirl the preserves into the finished ice cream. Take care not to overswirl or the preserves will "melt" into the ice cream. Streaks of preserves should be visible. Serve immediately or freeze until firm.

APPLE BUTTER ICE CREAM

MAKES ABOUT 1 QUART

ALTHOUGH apple butter can be found wherever you buy jam and jelly, look for unsweetened and unspiced apple butter. If you have trouble finding it, call Central Market in Austin, Texas (800-360-2552).

1 cup sugar

2 large eggs

2 large egg yolks

2 teaspoons all-purpose
flour

2 cups light cream

1½ cups unsweetened,
unspiced apple butter

½ teaspoon ground
cinnamon

½ teaspoon vanilla extract

In a medium mixing bowl, beat the sugar into the eggs and egg yolks until thickened and pale yellow. Beat in the flour. Set aside.

Bring the light cream to a simmer in a heavy medium saucepan. Slowly beat the hot cream into the eggs and sugar. Pour the entire mixture back into the pan and place over low heat. Stir constantly with a whisk or wooden spoon until the custard thickens slightly. Be careful not to let the mixture boil or the eggs will scramble. Remove from the heat and whisk in the apple butter and cinnamon. Pour the hot apple butter custard through a strainer into a large, clean bowl. Stir in the vanilla. Cool to room temperature, then cover and refrigerate until cold or overnight.

Stir the chilled custard, then freeze in 1 or 2 batches in your ice cream machine according to the manufacturer's instructions. When finished, the ice cream will be soft but ready to eat. For firmer ice cream, transfer to a freezer-safe container and freeze at least 2 hours.

Serving Tip: Hollow out an apple and fill with apple butter ice cream. Serve on a small dessert plate dusted with ground cinnamon.

Variations

APPLE BROWN BETTY ICE CREAM Substitute ½ cup dark brown sugar for ½ cup of the granulated sugar. Add ½ cup crumbled ginger snaps to the machine when the ice cream is semifrozen. Allow the machine to mix in the cookies. Proceed with the recipe as directed.

APPLE CHEDDAR ICE CREAM
Add ½ cup finely grated sharp Cheddar cheese to the machine when the ice cream is semifrozen. Allow the machine to mix in the cheese. Proceed with the recipe as directed.

APPLE CHERRY SWIRL ICE CREAM
Swirl ½ cup canned cherry pie filling into the finished ice cream. Take care not to overswirl or the filling will "melt" into the ice cream. Streaks of cherry sauce should be visible. Serve immediately or freeze until firm.

APPLE CINNAMON COFFEE CAKE ICE CREAM
Add ¼ cup chocolate chips and ½ cup crumbled coffee cake to the machine when the ice cream is semifrozen. Allow the machine to mix in the additional ingredients. Proceed with the recipe as directed.

APPLE PIE ICE CREAM
Add ¼ teaspoon ground nutmeg and ⅛ teaspoon ground mace to the custard along with the vanilla. If desired, add ½ cup crumbled baked pie crust to the machine when the ice cream is semifrozen. Allow the machine to mix in the crust. Proceed with the recipe as directed.

APPLE RAISIN WALNUT ICE CREAM
Add ¼ cup raisins and ¼ cup walnuts to the machine when the ice cream is semifrozen. Allow the machine to mix in the additional ingredients. Proceed with the recipe as directed.

APPLE THYME ICE CREAM
Omit the cinnamon and add 1 tablespoon chopped fresh thyme to the custard along with the vanilla. Proceed with the recipe as directed.

APRICOT ICE CREAM

MAKES ABOUT 1 QUART

FRESH apricots are fine for eating, but their flavor can be too delicate for ice cream. Dried apricots—Turkish or California, sulfured or unsulfured—have an intense flavor that cuts through the cream.

6 ounces dried apricot
    halves (about 1 cup
    loosely packed)
3 tablespoons light corn
    syrup
½ teaspoon salt
¾ cup sugar
4 large egg yolks
1 cup half-and-half
1½ cups heavy cream
1 teaspoon vanilla extract

Cover the apricot halves with boiling water and let sit for 1 hour or until soft. Drain the apricots, then combine with the corn syrup and salt in a food processor. Blend until very smooth, about 2 minutes. Set aside.

In a medium bowl, beat the sugar into the egg yolks until they are thickened and pale yellow. Set aside.

Bring the half-and-half to a simmer in a heavy medium saucepan. Slowly beat the hot half-and-half into the eggs and sugar. Pour the entire mixture back into the pan and place over low heat. Stir constantly with a whisk or wooden spoon until the custard thickens slightly. Be careful not to let the mixture boil or the eggs will scramble. Remove from the heat and whisk in the apricot puree. Pour the hot apricot custard through a strainer into a large, clean bowl. The custard will be thick and may need to be rubbed through the strainer with the back of a wooden spoon. You may also strain the hot custard through a food mill. Allow the custard to cool slightly, then stir in the cream and vanilla. Cover and refrigerate until cold or overnight.

Stir the chilled custard, then freeze in 1 or 2 batches in your ice cream machine according to the manufacturer's instructions. When finished, the ice cream will be soft but ready to eat. For firmer ice cream, transfer to a freezer-safe container and freeze at least 2 hours.

continued

Variations

APRICOT HAZELNUT ICE CREAM Add ½ cup chopped toasted hazelnuts (see page xvi) to the machine when the ice cream is semifrozen. Allow the machine to mix in the nuts. Proceed with the recipe as directed.

CHOCOLATE-DIPPED APRICOT ICE CREAM Gently swirl ½ cup chocolate syrup or sauce into the finished ice cream. Be careful not to overswirl or the chocolate will "melt" into the ice cream. Streaks of chocolate should be visible. Serve immediately or freeze until firm.

DRUNKEN APRICOT ICE CREAM Add ¼ cup dark rum to the custard before freezing. Proceed with the recipe as directed.

PARISIAN APRICOT ICE CREAM Cover the apricots with warm brandy instead of water. Proceed with the recipe as directed.

SPICED APRICOT ICE CREAM Add ½ teaspoon ground cinnamon, ¼ teaspoon ground nutmeg, and ⅛ teaspoon ground mace to the custard along with the vanilla. Proceed with the recipe as directed.

AVOCADO ICE CREAM AND GAZPACHO

MAKES ABOUT 3 CUPS

WHEN I first tasted avocado ice cream, I knew I was on to something. When I tasted it in a bowl of crunchy, spicy gazpacho, I knew it was something special. This unusual combination makes a wonderful midsummer lunch, a refreshing afternoon snack, or an elegant first course for dinner.

2 ripe, soft avocados,
   about ½ pound each

½ cup sour cream

3 tablespoons lime juice

⅔ cup sugar

½ teaspoon salt

1 fresh jalapeño, seeded,
   veined, and roughly
   chopped (optional)

1 cup light cream

Peel and pit the avocados. Roughly chop the avocados and place in a food processor along with the sour cream, lime juice, sugar, salt, and jalapeño. Process until smooth. Transfer the puree to a medium mixing bowl and stir in the cream. Cover and refrigerate until well chilled.

Stir the chilled mixture, then freeze in your ice cream machine according to the manufacturer's instructions. When finished, transfer the soft ice cream to a freezer-safe container and freeze at least 2 hours, or until firm.

To serve, place 1 scoop of ice cream in a chilled bowl of gazpacho.

GAZPACHO

MAKES ABOUT 6 CUPS

Combine all the ingredients in a medium bowl and mix well. Cover and refrigerate at least 6 hours. This soup can be made up to 3 days in advance.

3 cups tomato juice

2 tablespoons red wine
   vinegar

2 tablespoons lemon juice

1 teaspoon Worcestershire
   sauce

¼ teaspoon chili sauce

1 cup vegetable broth

1 cup minced celery

2 tablespoons minced onion

1 teaspoon minced garlic

1 small cucumber, peeled,
   seeded, and finely
   chopped

1 small green bell pepper,
   seeded, and finely
   chopped

½ teaspoon salt

¼ teaspoon freshly ground
   black pepper

BANANA ICE CREAM

MAKES ABOUT 1 QUART

FOR the strongest banana flavor, look for very ripe bananas with no green patches. A few brown spots are OK, since it means the sweetest banana taste is inside. Adding the banana liqueur can also intensify the flavor.

⅔ cup sugar

2 large eggs

1½ tablespoons all-purpose
   flour

⅛ teaspoon salt

1¼ cups milk

2 large, very ripe bananas

1 cup light cream

1 teaspoon vanilla extract

2 tablespoons banana
   liqueur (optional)

In a medium mixing bowl, beat the sugar into the eggs until thickened and pale yellow. Beat in the flour and salt. Set aside.

Bring the milk to a boil in a heavy medium saucepan. Slowly beat the hot milk into the eggs and sugar. Pour the entire mixture back into the pan and place over low heat. Stir constantly with a whisk or wooden spoon until the custard thickens slightly. Be careful not to let the mixture boil or the eggs will scramble. Remove from the heat and pour the hot custard through a strainer into a large, clean bowl.

Mash the bananas with the back of a fork until they are creamy, or puree them in a food processor. Add the banana puree to the hot custard and mix well. Allow the banana custard to cool slightly. Stir in the cream, vanilla, and liqueur, if using. Cover and refrigerate until cold or overnight.

Stir the chilled custard, then freeze in 1 or 2 batches in your ice cream machine according to the manufacturer's instructions. When finished, the ice cream will be soft but ready to eat. For firmer ice cream, transfer to a freezer-safe container and freeze at least 2 hours.

Variations

BANANA CANDY BAR ICE CREAM Add ½ cup chopped Snickers bars to the machine when the ice cream is semifrozen. Allow the machine to mix in the candy. Proceed with the recipe as directed.

BANANA CHOCOLATE CHIP ICE CREAM Add ½ cup bittersweet or milk chocolate chips or shavings to the machine when the ice cream is semifrozen. Allow the machine to mix in the chocolate. Proceed with the recipe as directed. (To create chocolate shavings, place the chocolate bar or square in the refrigerator to chill, then use a vegetable peeler to "shave" the chocolate.)

BANANA COCONUT ICE CREAM Substitute coconut milk for the dairy milk. Proceed with the recipe as directed, adding ½ cup toasted sweetened coconut (see page xvi) to the machine when the ice cream is semifrozen. Allow the machine to mix in the coconut. Proceed with the recipe as directed.

BANANA COOKIE ICE CREAM Add ½ cup crumbled chocolate creme cookies or ginger snaps to the machine when the ice cream is semifrozen. Allow the machine to mix in the cookies. Proceed with the recipe as directed.

BANANA DAIQUIRI ICE CREAM Add ¼ cup dark rum and 1 tablespoon bottled sweetened lime juice to the custard before freezing. Proceed with the recipe as directed.

BANANA NUT ICE CREAM Add ¼ teaspoon ground cinnamon to the custard along with the vanilla. Add ½ cup chopped pecans to the machine when the ice cream is semifrozen. Allow the machine to mix in the nuts. Proceed with the recipe as directed.

TROPICAL BANANA CRUNCH ICE CREAM Add ½ cup Grape-Nuts cereal and ¼ cup chopped toasted cashews (see page xvi) to the machine when the ice cream is semifrozen. Allow the machine to mix in the additional ingredients. Proceed with the recipe as directed.

BANANA ICE CREAM, PHILADELPHIA STYLE

THIS ice cream is easy to make but will only be as flavorful as the bananas you use. Pick the ripest ones you can find or set a couple of bananas in a brown paper bag overnight to help them ripen faster.

1½ cups light cream

⅔ cup sugar

2 ripe medium bananas

¼ cup half-and-half

2 tablespoons banana

    liqueur or syrup (optional)

Heat the cream in a heavy medium saucepan over medium heat until small bubbles appear around the edge. Do not let the cream boil. Remove from the heat. Add the sugar and stir until it dissolves completely. Cool to room temperature.

Cut the bananas into thin slices and place in a blender with the half-and-half and banana liqueur, if using. Blend until the bananas are pureed, about 15 seconds. Stir the banana puree into the cooled cream. Refrigerate until cold or overnight.

Stir the cream well, then freeze in 1 or 2 batches in your ice cream machine according to the manufacturer's instructions. When finished, the ice cream will be soft but ready to eat. For firmer ice cream, transfer to a freezer-safe container and freeze at least 2 hours.

◄ • ►

Variations

AMBROSIA ICE CREAM When the ice cream is semifrozen, add ¼ cup each of the following: toasted sweetened coconut (see page xvi), drained mandarin orange sections, and slivered almonds. Allow the machine to mix in the additional ingredients. Proceed with the recipe as directed.

BANANA BLUEBERRY ICE CREAM Mix ½ cup blueberries with 2 tablespoons sugar and 2 tablespoons dark rum. Let the fruit macerate at least 2 hours. Add this mixture to the cream before freezing. Proceed with the recipe as directed.

BANANA CREAM PIE ICE CREAM Add ½ cup crumbled vanilla cream wafer cookies to the machine when the ice cream is semifrozen. Allow the machine to mix in the cookies. Proceed with the recipe as directed.

BANANA FUDGE ICE CREAM Add ½ cup crumbled chocolate fudge or chocolate fudge cookies to the machine when the ice cream is semifrozen. Allow the machine to mix in the fudge. Proceed with the recipe as directed.

BANANA MALT ICE CREAM Stir ¼ cup malted milk powder into the cream along with the sugar. Proceed with the recipe as directed.

BANANA TART ICE CREAM Add ¼ cup crumbled ginger snaps to the machine when the ice cream is semifrozen. Allow the machine to stir in the cookies. Swirl ¼ cup caramel sauce into the finished ice cream. Take care not to overswirl or the sauce will "melt" into the ice cream. Streaks of caramel should be visible. Serve immediately or freeze until firm. Serve immediately or freeze until firm.

BUBBLE GUM ICE CREAM

BUBBLE gum flavoring is available from baking and candy-making suppliers, such as Sweet Celebrations in Edina, Minnesota (800-328-6722).

¾ cup sugar

3 large eggs

1 tablespoon cornstarch

1½ cups milk

1 cup heavy cream

2 teaspoons bubble gum
flavoring (.25 ounce
bottle)

In a medium mixing bowl, beat the sugar into the eggs until thickened and pale yellow. Beat in the cornstarch. Set aside.

Bring the milk to a simmer in a heavy medium saucepan. Slowly beat the hot milk into the eggs and sugar. Pour the entire mixture back into the pan and place over low heat. Stir constantly with a whisk or wooden spoon until the custard thickens slightly. Be careful not to let the mixture boil or the eggs will scramble. Remove from the heat and pour the hot custard through a strainer into a large, clean bowl. Allow the custard to cool slightly, then stir in the cream and bubble gum flavoring. Cover and refrigerate until cold or overnight.

Stir the chilled custard, then freeze in 1 or 2 batches in your ice cream machine according to the manufacturer's instructions. When finished, the ice cream will be soft but ready to eat. For firmer ice cream, transfer to a freezer-safe container and freeze at least 2 hours.

◂ • ▸

Variations

DOUBLE BUBBLE GUM ICE CREAM Add 2 tablespoons tiny candy-coated gum to the machine when the ice cream is semifrozen. Let the machine mix in the gum. Proceed with the recipe as directed.

SALT WATER TAFFY ICE CREAM Substitute taffy flavoring for bubble gum flavoring. Proceed with the recipe as directed, adding ½ cup chopped saltwater taffy to the machine when the ice cream is semifrozen. Allow the machine to mix in the candy. Proceed with the recipe as directed.

TUTTI-FRUTTI ICE CREAM Substitute tutti-frutti flavoring for bubble gum flavoring. Proceed with the recipe as directed, adding ½ cup chopped candied fruit to the machine when the ice cream is semifrozen. Allow the machine to mix in the fruit. Proceed with the recipe as directed.

BURNT SUGAR ICE CREAM

SUGAR caramelizes at temperatures over 350°F, so it's important to be very careful when you're making this ice cream. Warming the milk before you add it to the burnt sugar helps control any splattering.

2 cups plus
1½ tablespoons milk
1½ cups sugar
1 tablespoon cornstarch
¼ teaspoon salt
3 large egg yolks
1 cup heavy cream
1 teaspoon vanilla extract

Place 2 cups of the milk in a small saucepan and bring to a simmer over low heat. Cover and keep warm while caramelizing the sugar.

Place the sugar in a large, heavy saucepan with high sides over medium heat. Stir with a whisk or wooden spoon until the sugar dissolves. Continue to cook without stirring until the sugar turns golden brown. Immediately remove the pot from the heat. Very carefully and slowly add the warmed milk, stirring constantly. The mixture will rise, foam, and splatter. The sugar may also harden into a lump on the bottom of the pan. Return the pan to low heat and stir until the caramel has dissolved into the milk. Keep warm over very low heat.

In a small mixing bowl, mix the cornstarch and salt with the remaining 1½ tablespoons of milk. Stir until smooth, then beat into the egg yolks in a medium bowl. Slowly beat the hot milk and sugar into the egg yolk mixture. Pour the entire mixture back into the pan and place over low heat. Stir constantly with a whisk or wooden spoon until the custard thickens slightly. Be careful not to let the mixture boil or the eggs will scramble. Remove from the heat and pour the hot burnt sugar custard through a strainer into a large, clean bowl. Allow the custard to cool slightly, then stir in the cream and vanilla. Cover and refrigerate until cold or overnight.

Stir the chilled custard, then freeze in 1 or 2 batches in your ice cream machine according to the manufacturer's instructions. When finished, the ice cream will be soft but ready to eat. For firmer ice cream, transfer to a freezer-safe container and freeze at least 2 hours.

Variations

BURNT SUGAR PIE ICE CREAM Add ½ cup crumbled graham crackers and ½ cup mini-marshmallows to the machine when the ice cream is semifrozen. Allow the machine to mix in the additional ingredients. Proceed with the recipe as directed.

COCONUT CRÈME BRÛLÉE ICE CREAM Add ½ cup toasted sweetened coconut (see page xvi) to the machine when the ice cream is semifrozen. Allow the machine to mix in the coconut. Proceed with the recipe as directed.

CRÈME ANGLAISE ICE CREAM Increase the vanilla to 3 tablespoons. Proceed with the recipe as directed.

ORANGE CRÈME BRÛLÉE ICE CREAM Add 2 teaspoons grated orange zest and 2 tablespoons orange liqueur (optional) along with the vanilla. Proceed with the recipe as directed.

RASPBERRY CRÈME BRÛLÉE ICE CREAM Mix 2 tablespoons water into ½ cup raspberry jam to help loosen it up. Gently swirl the jam into the finished ice cream. Be careful not to overswirl or the jam will "melt" into the ice cream. Streaks of jam should be visible. Serve immediately or freeze until firm.

VERSAILLES CRÈME BRÛLÉE ICE CREAM Add 2 tablespoons Cognac and ¼ cup chopped toasted walnuts (see page xvi) before freezing. Proceed with the recipe as directed.

BUTTER PECAN ICE CREAM

MAKES ABOUT 5 CUPS

BUTTER pecan ice cream is an absolute classic. Adding Red Pepper–Pecan Praline Crunch (recipe follows) instead of plain pecans turns it into an absolute original. The spice of the chiles and the sweet creaminess of the ice cream are a combination made only in heaven . . . and Texas.

2 large eggs

3 tablespoons unsalted butter

⅔ cup packed dark brown sugar

½ cup half-and-half

2 cups light cream

1 teaspoon vanilla extract

¼ teaspoon almond extract

1½ cups pecan halves

Put the eggs in a medium bowl and set aside. Melt the butter in a heavy medium saucepan over low heat. Heat until the butter begins to turns golden brown and smells mildly of nuts. Add the brown sugar, stirring until it melts. Stir in the half-and-half and bring to a simmer. Slowly beat the hot half-and-half mixture into the eggs. Return the entire mixture to the pan and place over low heat. Stir constantly with a whisk or wooden spoon until the custard thickens slightly. Be careful not to let the mixture boil or the eggs will scramble. Remove from the heat and pour the hot custard through a strainer into a large, clean bowl. Allow the custard to cool slightly, then stir in the cream, vanilla, and almond extract. Cover and refrigerate until cold or overnight.

Stir the chilled custard, then freeze in 1 or 2 batches in your ice cream machine according to the manufacturer's instructions, adding the pecans to the machine when the ice cream is semifrozen. Allow the machine to mix in the nuts. When finished, the ice cream will be soft but ready to eat. For firmer ice cream, transfer to a freezer-safe container and freeze at least 2 hours.

‹ • ›

Variations

BUTTER FRUITCAKE ICE CREAM Substitute 1½ cups crumbled fruitcake (with nuts) for the pecans. Proceed with the recipe as directed.

GINGER BUTTER PECAN ICE CREAM Add 2 tablespoons finely chopped crystallized ginger and ¼ cup crumbled ginger snaps to the machine when the ice cream is semifrozen. Allow the machine to mix in the additional ingredients. Proceed with the recipe as directed.

PECAN PIE ICE CREAM Substitute maple syrup for the brown sugar and add ½ cup crumbled, baked frozen pie crust to the machine when the ice cream is semifrozen. Allow the machine to mix in the crust. Proceed with the recipe as directed.

PRALINE CHILE CRUNCH ICE CREAM Substitute 1½ cups Red Pepper–Pecan Praline Crunch (recipe follows) for the pecans. Proceed with the recipe as directed.

RED PEPPER–PECAN PRALINE CRUNCH

MAKES ABOUT 2 CUPS

1 cup sugar

½ cup water

1 cup pecan halves

2 teaspoons crushed red
pepper flakes

Because the fumes from the red peppers can cause your eyes and nose to burn, work in a well-ventilated kitchen.

Combine the sugar and water in a heavy medium saucepan. Place over medium heat and stir until the sugar dissolves. Continue to cook until the sugar turns light amber. Immediately remove from the heat and stir in the pecans and red pepper flakes. The hot sugar will release the red pepper oils, so be very careful to keep your face away from the pan. Stir vigorously to coat each nut, then turn out onto a marble slab or greased nonstick cookie sheet. Spread the nuts using 2 greased wooden spoons or spatulas, separating the nuts as much as possible. When completely cool, use a heavy knife to chop the nuts into ¼-inch pieces.

CANNOLI ICE CREAM

MAKES ABOUT 1 QUART

Cannoli are small Italian pastries with a ricotta filling, scented with lemon, anise, and vanilla. This ice cream is delicious on its own, or mixed with crumbled cannoli shells.

¾ cup sugar

2 large eggs

1 cup milk

½ teaspoon anise seeds, crushed

1½ cups ricotta (15-ounce container)

1 teaspoon grated fresh lemon zest

1 teaspoon vanilla extract

1 cup heavy cream

2 cups crumbled cannoli shells (optional; recipe follows)

In a medium mixing bowl, beat the sugar into the eggs until thickened and pale yellow. Set aside.

Combine the milk and anise seeds in a heavy medium saucepan. Bring to a simmer over low heat. Slowly beat the hot milk into the eggs and sugar.

Pour the entire mixture back into the pan and place over low heat. Stir constantly with a whisk or wooden spoon until the custard thickens slightly. Be careful not to let the mixture boil or the eggs will scramble. Remove from the heat and whisk in the ricotta. Pour the hot ricotta custard through a strainer into a large, clean bowl. Allow the custard to cool slightly, then stir in the lemon zest, vanilla, and cream. Cover and refrigerate until cold or overnight.

Stir the chilled custard, then freeze in 1 or 2 batches in your ice cream machine according to the manufacturer's instructions, adding the crumbled cannoli shells when the ice cream is semifrozen. Allow the machine to mix in the crumbled pastry. When finished, the ice cream will be soft but ready to eat. For firmer ice cream, transfer to a freezer-safe container and freeze at least 2 hours.

CANNOLI SHELLS

1 large egg white

2 tablespoons water

1¼ cups all-purpose flour

1 tablespoon sugar

¼ teaspoon salt

1 tablespoon unsalted
   butter, melted

Vegetable oil, for deep-
   frying

In a small mixing bowl, lightly beat the egg white with the water. Sift the flour, sugar, and salt into a large bowl. Make a well in the center. Pour the egg white and the butter into the well. Slowly incorporate the flour into the liquid, using a fork. Mix until a dough comes together. Knead the dough on a floured board for 2 minutes or until the dough is smooth but not hard. Wrap in plastic and refrigerate at least 2 hours.

Roll out the dough on a floured surface into a rectangle about ⅛ inch thick. Use a paring knife to cut the dough into 6-inch squares. (Since the shells are crumbled, there's no need to make the traditional cannoli shape.) Pour the oil into a heavy frying pan to a depth of 1 inch. Heat the oil to 350°F and carefully lower the pastries into the hot oil. Cook 2 at a time, until golden brown, about 5 minutes. Remove with a slotted spoon and drain on paper towels. Allow to cool before storing in an airtight container until ready for use.

CANDIED CANNOLI ICE CREAM Add ¼ cup candied fruit to the machine when the ice cream is semifrozen. Allow the machine to mix in the fruit. Proceed with the recipe as directed.

CHOCOLATE CANNOLI ICE CREAM Omit the anise seeds and lemon zest. Add ½ cup miniature chocolate chips to the machine when the ice cream is semifrozen. Allow the machine to mix in the chips. Proceed with the recipe as indicated.

TORRONE ICE CREAM Omit the anise seeds. Substitute ½ cup honey for ½ cup of the sugar. Add ¼ cup slivered almonds to the machine when the ice cream is semifrozen. Allow the machine to mix in the nuts. Proceed with the recipe as directed.

CASHEW ICE CREAM

NOTHING tops off this sweet, nutty ice cream like a handful of salted cashews. Or a few raisins, a handful of trail mix, some crumbled peanut brittle . . .

Warm the cashews in a small sauté pan over low heat. Shake the pan or stir often, being careful not to let the nuts burn. After about 2 minutes, or when the nuts smell fragrant, add the corn syrup and heat only until the syrup is warmed through. Scrape the nuts and syrup into a food processor and process for 1 minute or until the cashews are completely smooth. Add the eggs and process until well blended, about 30 seconds.

1½ cups toasted unsalted cashews (see page xvi)

¼ cup light corn syrup

2 large eggs, at room temperature

1½ cups milk

¾ cup sugar

1 cup heavy cream

½ teaspoon vanilla extract

Combine the milk and sugar in a heavy medium saucepan. Place over medium heat and stir until the sugar dissolves and the milk comes to a boil. With the food processor running, slowly pour the hot milk through the feed tube.

Process 30 seconds or until the nut custard is smooth. Pour the entire mixture back into the pan and place over low heat. Stir constantly with a whisk or wooden spoon until the custard thickens slightly. Be careful not to let the mixture boil or the eggs will scramble. Remove from the heat and pour the hot cashew custard through a strainer into a large, clean bowl. Allow the custard to cool slightly, then stir in the cream and vanilla. Cover and refrigerate until cold or overnight.

Stir the chilled custard, then freeze in 1 or 2 batches in your ice cream machine according to the manufacturer's instructions. When finished, the ice cream will be soft but ready to eat. For firmer ice cream, transfer to a freezer-safe container and freeze at least 2 hours.

Variations

KUNG PAO CASHEW ICE CREAM Add 1 teaspoon crushed red pepper flakes along with the vanilla. Proceed with the recipe as directed.

RAIN FOREST CRUNCH ICE CREAM When the ice cream is semifrozen, add to the machine ¼ cup each chopped salted cashews, chopped salted brazil nuts, and toasted sweetened coconut (see page xvi). Allow the machine to mix in the additional ingredients. Proceed with the recipe as directed.

TRAIL MIX ICE CREAM Add ¼ cup toasted sweetened coconut (see page xvi), ¼ cup sunflower seeds, and ¼ cup raisins to the machine when the ice cream is semifrozen. Allow the machine to mix in the additional ingredients. Proceed with the recipe as directed.

CHEESECAKE ICE CREAM

JUST like any great cheesecake, this ice cream is better the next day.

1 cup sugar

4 ounces cream cheese, at
room temperature

1 large egg

½ teaspoon vanilla extract

¾ cup milk

2 teaspoons grated fresh
lemon or orange zest

1½ cups heavy cream

3 graham crackers,
crumbled

Beat the sugar and the cream cheese together until smooth and creamy. Beat in the egg and vanilla. Set aside.

Bring the milk to a boil in a heavy medium saucepan. Slowly beat the hot milk into the cheese mixture. Pour the entire mixture back into the pan and place over low heat. Stir constantly with a whisk or wooden spoon until the custard thickens slightly. Be careful not to let the mixture boil or the egg will scramble. Remove from the heat and pour the hot cheese custard through a strainer into a large, clean bowl. Allow the custard to cool slightly, then stir in the lemon zest and cream. Cover and refrigerate until cold or overnight.

Stir the chilled custard, then freeze in 1 or 2 batches in your ice cream machine according to the manufacturer's instructions, adding the crumbled graham crackers to the machine when the ice cream is semifrozen. Allow the machine to mix in the crackers. When finished, the ice cream will be soft but ready to eat. For firmer ice cream, transfer to a freezer-safe container and freeze at least 2 hours.

‹ • ›

Variations

CHERRY CHEESECAKE ICE CREAM Gently swirl ¾ cup canned cherry pie filling into the finished ice cream. Be careful not to overswirl or the cherries will "melt" into the ice cream. Streaks of cherry "sauce" should be visible. Serve immediately or freeze until firm.

LEMON POPPY SEED CHEESECAKE ICE CREAM Add 2 teaspoons poppy seeds to the custard along with the vanilla. Proceed with the recipe as directed. Gently swirl ¾ cup cold lemon curd or canned lemon pie filling into the finished ice cream. Be careful not to overswirl or the sauce will "dissolve" into the ice cream. Streaks of lemon sauce should be visible. Serve immediately or freeze until firm.

MINT CHOCOLATE CHIP CHEESECAKE ICE CREAM Omit the lemon zest. Substitute peppermint extract for the vanilla extract. Add ½ cup miniature chocolate chips to the machine when the ice cream is semifrozen. Allow the machine to mix in the chips. Proceed with the recipe as directed.

OREO CHEESECAKE ICE CREAM Omit the lemon zest. Substitute crumbled Oreos for the graham crackers. Proceed with the recipe as directed.

WHITE CHOCOLATE CHEESECAKE ICE CREAM Omit the lemon zest. Add ½ cup melted white chocolate to the custard along with the vanilla. Proceed with the recipe as directed.

CHERRY ICE CREAM

FRESH, frozen, or canned cherries all work well in the recipe, so you can enjoy this classic ice cream any time of the year.

¾ cup sugar

3 large egg yolks

1 tablespoon all-purpose
flour

1 cup half-and-half

¾ pound fresh or frozen
Bing cherries, pitted and
chopped, or one
16-ounce can pitted
sweet cherries, drained
and chopped

¼ cup cherry syrup

1½ cups heavy cream

In a medium mixing bowl, beat the sugar into the egg yolks until thickened and pale yellow. Beat in the flour and set aside.

Bring the half-and-half to a simmer in a heavy medium saucepan. Slowly beat the hot half-and-half into the eggs and sugar. Pour the entire mixture back into the pan and place over low heat. Stir constantly with a whisk or wooden spoon until the custard thickens slightly. Be careful not to let the mixture boil or the eggs will scramble. Remove from the heat and pour the hot custard through a strainer into a large, clean bowl. Allow the custard to cool slightly, then stir in the chopped cherries, cherry syrup, and cream. Cover and refrigerate until cold or overnight.

Stir the chilled custard, then freeze in 1 or 2 batches in your ice cream machine according to the manufacturer's instructions. When finished, the ice cream will be soft but ready to eat. For firmer ice cream, transfer to a freezer-safe container and freeze at least 2 hours.

‹ • ›

Variations

CHERRY BANANA ICE CREAM Slice 1 large banana into ¼-inch pieces. Toss with 2 tablespoons sugar and 2 tablespoons brandy or banana liqueur. Let macerate at least 2 hours. Add this mixture to the custard along with the cherry syrup. Proceed with the recipe as directed.

CHERRY CANDY BAR ICE CREAM Add ½ cup chopped chocolate-covered peppermint candies to the machine when the ice cream is semifrozen. Allow the machine to mix in the candy. Proceed with the recipe as directed.

CHERRY CORDIAL ICE CREAM Substitute ¼ cup cherry brandy or cherry liqueur for the cherry syrup. Proceed with the recipe as directed.

CHERRY PIE ICE CREAM Add ¼ teaspoon almond extract along with the cherry syrup. Add ½ cup crumbled sugar cookies or baked pie crust to the machine when the ice cream is semifrozen. Allow the machine to mix in the cookies. Proceed with the recipe as directed.

CHERRY SEED ICE CREAM Add ½ cup chopped unsalted sunflower seeds to the machine when the ice cream is semifrozen. Allow the machine to mix in the seeds. Proceed with the recipe as directed.

CHOCOLATE-COVERED CHERRY ICE CREAM Swirl ½ cup chocolate syrup or chocolate sauce into the finished ice cream. Take care not to overswirl or the chocolate will "melt" into the ice cream. Streaks of chocolate should be visible. Serve immediately or freeze until firm.

CHERRY ICE CREAM, PHILADELPHIA STYLE

THIS ice cream requires fresh cherries. Remove all the pits before adding the pureed cherries to the cream.

½ cup heavy cream

⅓ cup sugar

1 cup stemmed and pitted
    fresh sweet cherries

¼ cup sweet cherry or
    black cherry syrup

Heat the cream in a heavy medium saucepan over medium heat, until small bubbles appear around the edge. Do not let the cream boil. Remove from the heat and add the sugar, stirring until the sugar dissolves completely. Cool to room temperature.

Place the cherries in a blender with the cherry syrup and blend until the fruit is pureed, about 15 seconds. Stir the cherry puree into the cooled cream. Refrigerate until cold or overnight.

Freeze in 1 or 2 batches in your ice cream machine according to the manufacturer's instructions. When finished, the ice cream will be soft but ready to eat. For firmer ice cream, transfer to a freezer-safe container and freeze for at least 4 hours.

◄ • ►

Variations

CHERRY CHOCOLATE NUT ICE CREAM Add ¼ cup shaved semisweet chocolate and ¼ cup chopped toasted pecans (see page xvi) to the machine when the ice cream is semi-frozen. Allow the machine to mix in the additional ingredients. Proceed with the recipe as indicated.

CHERRY LICORICE ICE CREAM Add 1 tablespoon crushed fennel seeds to the cream before heating. Proceed with the recipe as directed.

CHERRY LIME RICKEY ICE CREAM Add 2 teaspoons grated fresh lime zest and 1 tablespoon bottled sweetened lime juice along with the cherries. Proceed with the recipe as indicated.

CHERRY MALTED ICE CREAM Add ¼ cup malted milk powder along with the sugar. Proceed with the recipe as directed.

CHESTNUT ICE CREAM

MAKES ABOUT 1 QUART

Y OU can make this ice cream using whole chestnuts, but unsweetened chestnut puree makes it smoother and creamier. If you can't find unsweetened chestnut puree in your market, call Central Market in Austin, Texas (800-360-2552).

one 8-ounce can
 unsweetened chestnut
 puree
one 15-ounce can
 sweetened condensed
 milk
2 large eggs
⅛ teaspoon salt
2 cups half-and-half
1 teaspoon vanilla extract

Place the chestnut puree in a food processor with the sweetened condensed milk and process for 2 minutes or until the mixture is smooth and creamy. Add the eggs and salt. Process until well incorporated, about 1 minute.

Bring the half-and-half to a boil in a heavy medium saucepan. With the food processor running, slowly pour the hot half-and-half into the chestnut puree through the feed tube. Process until well blended. Pour the entire mixture back into the pan and place over low heat. Stir constantly with a whisk or wooden spoon until the custard thickens slightly. Be careful not to let the mixture boil or the eggs will scramble. Remove from the heat and pour the hot chestnut custard through a strainer into a large, clean bowl. Allow the custard to cool slightly, then stir in the vanilla. Cover and refrigerate until cold or overnight.

Stir the chilled custard, then freeze in 1 or 2 batches in your ice cream machine according to the manufacturer's instructions. When finished, the ice cream will be soft but ready to eat. For firmer ice cream, transfer to a freezer-safe container and freeze at least 2 hours.

‹ • ›

Variations

CHRISTMAS TREAT ICE CREAM Add ½ teaspoon ground cinnamon along with the sweetened condensed milk. Proceed with the recipe as directed. Add ¼ cup candied fruit to the machine when the ice cream is semifrozen. Allow the machine to mix in the fruit. Continue with the recipe as directed.

continued

GINGER CHESTNUT ICE CREAM Add 2 tablespoons finely chopped crystallized ginger and ½ cup crumbled ginger snaps to the machine when the ice cream is semifrozen. Allow the machine to mix in the additional ingredients. Proceed with the recipe as directed.

HONEY CHESTNUT ICE CREAM Add ¼ cup honey along with the sweetened condensed milk. Proceed with the recipe as directed. Note: this ice cream is very delicious but very sweet.

LOUIS XIV ICE CREAM Roughly chop ½ cup pitted sweet cherries and 3 pitted fresh apricots. Toss with 2 tablespoons sugar and 2 tablespoons Cognac. Allow the fruit to macerate at least 2 hours. Add this mixture to the custard before freezing. Proceed with the recipe as indicated.

MARRON GLACÉ ICE CREAM Add ½ cup chopped candied chestnuts to the machine when the ice cream is semifrozen. Allow the machine to mix in the nuts. Proceed with the recipe as directed.

MONT BLANC ICE CREAM Swirl ½ cup chocolate syrup and ½ cup marshmallow creme into the finished ice cream. Take care not to overswirl or the sauces will "melt" into the ice cream. Streaks of marshmallow and chocolate should be visible. Serve immediately or freeze until firm.

NUTTY CHESTNUT ICE CREAM Add ½ cup toasted unsalted pumpkin seeds (see page xvi) to the machine when the ice cream is semifrozen. Allow the machine to mix in the seeds. Proceed with the recipe as indicated.

CHOCOLATE ICE CREAM

PURE and simple chocolate ice cream, this classic recipe speaks for itself.

1 cup sugar

3 large eggs

1 cup cocoa powder

1½ cups milk

1 cup heavy cream

1 tablespoon vanilla extract

Place the sugar, eggs, and cocoa in a food processor and blend until smooth.

Bring the milk to a boil in a heavy medium saucepan. With the food processor running, slowly pour the hot milk into the chocolate mixture through the feed tube. Process until well blended. Pour the entire mixture back into the pan and place over low heat. Stir constantly with a whisk or wooden spoon until the custard thickens slightly. Be careful not to let the mixture boil or the eggs will scramble. Remove from the heat and pour the hot chocolate custard through a strainer into a large, clean bowl. Allow the custard to cool slightly, then stir in the cream and vanilla. Cover and refrigerate until cold or overnight.

Stir the chilled custard, then freeze in 1 or 2 batches in your ice cream machine according to the manufacturer's instructions. When finished, the ice cream will be soft but ready to eat. For firmer ice cream, transfer to a freezer-safe container and freeze at least 2 hours.

‹ • ›

Variations

CHOCOLATE BANANA CHIP ICE CREAM Add ½ cup chopped dried banana chips to the machine when the ice cream is semifrozen. Allow the machine to mix in the chips. Proceed with the recipe as directed.

CHOCOLATE BRITTLE ICE CREAM Add ½ cup chopped peanut brittle to the machine when the ice cream is semifrozen. Allow the machine to mix in the candy. Proceed with the recipe as directed.

CHOCOLATE CANDY BAR ICE CREAM Add 2 chopped candy bars of your choice to the machine when the ice cream is semifrozen. Allow the machine to mix in the candy.

continued

Proceed with the recipe as directed. Candy bar suggestions include Snickers, Milky Way, Fifth Avenue, Clark Bar, Baby Ruth, Nestle Crunch, $100,000 Bar, KitKat, Butterfinger, Chunky, or Twix.

CHOCOLATE CANDY DISH ICE CREAM

Add ½ cup small candies of your choice to the machine when the ice cream is semifrozen. Allow the machine to mix in the candy. Proceed with the recipe as directed. Candy suggestions include M&M's, Goobers, Raisinettes, Reese's Pieces, or Junior Mints.

CHOCOLATE CHEESECAKE ICE CREAM

Stir in ½ cup no-bake cheesecake powder mix along with the cream and vanilla. Proceed with the recipe as directed. Optional: add 1 cup crumbled cheesecake to the machine when the ice cream is semifrozen. Allow the machine to mix the cake in.

CHOCOLATE COOKIE ICE CREAM

Add 1 cup crumbled chocolate chip cookies to the machine when the ice cream is semifrozen. Allow the machine to mix in the cookies. Proceed with the recipe as directed.

CHOCOLATE MARSHMALLOW NUT ICE CREAM

Add ½ cup mini-marshmallows and ½ cup chopped toasted almonds (see page xvi) to the machine when the ice cream is semifrozen. Allow the machine to mix in the additional ingredients. Proceed with the recipe as directed.

GERMAN CHOCOLATE ICE CREAM

Add ½ cup shredded sweetened coconut to the machine when the ice cream is semifrozen. Allow the machine to mix in the coconut. Proceed with the recipe as directed. Swirl ½ cup caramel sauce into the finished ice cream. Take care not to overswirl or the caramel will "melt" into the ice cream. Streaks of caramel should be visible. Serve immediately or freeze until firm.

MEXICAN CHOCOLATE-ALMOND ICE CREAM

Add ¼ teaspoon ground cinnamon to the food processor along with the eggs and cocoa. Add ¼ teaspoon almond extract along with the vanilla. Proceed with the recipe as directed. Add ½ cup chopped toasted almonds (see page xvi) to the machine when the ice cream is semifrozen. Allow the machine to mix in the nuts. Continue with the recipe as directed.

CHOCOLATE "LOWER-FAT" ICE CREAM

I N the world of chocolate ice cream, the adjective "low-fat" is relative. Sweetened condensed milk replaces heavy cream in this recipe, thereby reducing the fat content of the ice cream. Want to trim even more fat? Use skim milk and fat-free sweetened condensed milk. The texture will not be as rich, but the flavor will still be intense.

2 cups milk (2% milk or

   skim milk)

¼ cup cocoa powder

2 ounces unsweetened

   chocolate, chopped

2 large eggs

1 can sweetened

   condensed milk (low-fat

   or fat-free)

1 teaspoon vanilla extract

Bring the milk to a simmer in a heavy medium saucepan. Whisk in the cocoa and bring the milk back to a simmer. Simmer for 3 minutes, stirring constantly. Remove from the heat and add the chocolate. Stir until melted. Slowly beat the warm milk and chocolate into the eggs in a bowl. Return the whole mixture to the pan set over low heat. Stir constantly with a whisk or wooden spoon until the custard thickens slightly. Be careful not to let the mixture boil or the eggs will scramble. Remove from the heat and pour the hot chocolate custard through a strainer into a large, clean bowl. Stir in the sweetened condensed milk and vanilla. Cover and refrigerate until cold or overnight.

Stir the chilled custard, then freeze in 1 or 2 batches in your ice cream machine according to the manufacturer's instructions. When finished, the ice cream will be soft but ready to eat. For firmer ice cream, transfer to a freezer-safe container and freeze at least 2 hours.

◂ • ▸

Variations

CHOCOLATE CRUNCH ICE CREAM Add ½ cup Grape-Nuts cereal to the machine when the ice cream is semifrozen. Allow the machine to mix in the cereal. Proceed with the recipe as directed.

CHOCOLATE HALLOWEEN ICE CREAM Add ¼ cup unsalted pumpkin seeds to the machine when the ice cream is semifrozen. Allow the machine to mix in the seeds.

continued

Proceed with the recipe as directed. Then swirl ¾ cup canned sweetened pumpkin pie filling into the finished ice cream. Take care not to overswirl or the pumpkin will "melt" into the ice cream. Streaks of pumpkin should be visible. Serve immediately or freeze until firm.

CHOCOLATE MARSHMALLOW ICE CREAM Swirl 1 cup marshmallow creme into the finished ice cream. Take care not to overswirl or the marshmallow will "melt" into the ice cream. Streaks of marshmallow should be visible. Serve immediately or freeze until firm.

CHOCOLATE RAISIN ICE CREAM Add ½ cup raisins or chocolate-covered raisins to the machine when the ice cream is semifrozen. Allow the machine to mix in the candy. Proceed with the recipe as directed.

CHOCOLATE CHERRY ICE CREAM

MAKES ABOUT 1 QUART

WHILE fresh, frozen, or canned sweet red cherries blend perfectly with chocolate, you'll need to add cherry syrup to help the sweet flavor of the fruit come through. Look for cherry syrup in your supermarket near the ice cream toppings or call Zabar's in New York City (212-787-2000).

1 heaping cup pitted sweet
cherries

¼ cup cherry syrup

½ teaspoon vanilla extract

¾ cup sugar

⅓ cup unsweetened cocoa
powder

1½ cups half-and-half

1 large egg

¾ cup heavy cream

Puree the cherries with the cherry syrup and vanilla in a blender. Set aside.

Combine the sugar, cocoa, and half-and-half in a heavy medium saucepan. Place over low heat. Stir constantly until the mixture is well blended and comes to a simmer. Remove from the heat and slowly beat the hot half-and-half mixture into the egg. Pour the hot chocolate custard through a strainer into a large, clean bowl. Stir in the cherry puree and heavy cream. Cover and refrigerate until cold or overnight.

Stir the chilled custard, then freeze in 1 or 2 batches in your ice cream machine according to the manufacturer's instructions. When finished, the ice cream will be soft but ready to eat. For firmer ice cream, transfer to a freezer-safe container and freeze at least 2 hours.

◂ • ▸

Variations

CHOCOLATE CHERRY CORDIAL ICE CREAM Substitute cherry liqueur for cherry syrup. Proceed with the recipe as directed.

SOUTHERN CHOCOLATE CHERRY PIE ICE CREAM Add ¼ teaspoon almond extract along with the vanilla. Add ¼ cup chopped toasted almonds (see page xvi) and ½ cup crumbled graham crackers to the machine when the ice cream is semifrozen. Allow the machine to mix in the additional ingredients. Proceed with the recipe as directed.

CHOCOLATE MALT ICE CREAM

THIS recipe calls for four to six tablespoons of malted milk powder. If you want a milder malt flavor, use less. If you want a stronger taste, use more. Just keep in mind that the malt flavor lessens as the ice cream sits in your freezer.

3 ounces unsweetened baking chocolate, chopped

1 cup sugar

4 to 6 tablespoons malted milk powder

2 cups half-and-half

2 large eggs, lightly beaten

1 cup heavy cream

2 teaspoons vanilla extract

Combine the chopped chocolate, sugar, malted milk powder, and half-and-half in a heavy medium saucepan. Place over low heat and stir until the chocolate is completely melted and the sugar is dissolved. Bring the mixture to a simmer and cook for 1 minute, stirring constantly. Slowly beat the hot half-and-half mixture into the eggs in a bowl. Return the entire mixture back to the pan and place over low heat. Stir constantly with a whisk or wooden spoon until the custard thickens slightly. Be careful not to let the mixture boil or the eggs will scramble. Remove from the heat and pour the hot chocolate custard through a strainer into a large, clean bowl.

At this point the custard should be homogenous. If you see specks of chocolate, allow the custard to cool slightly, then pour the custard into a blender and blend for 30 seconds. Pour back into the bowl. Stir in the cream and vanilla. Cover and refrigerate until cold or overnight.

Stir the chilled custard, then freeze in 1 or 2 batches in your ice cream machine according to the manufacturer's instructions. When finished, the ice cream will be soft but ready to eat. For firmer ice cream, transfer to a freezer-safe container and freeze at least 2 hours.

Variations

CHOCOLATE BANANA MALT ICE CREAM Slice 2 small bananas thin. Toss with 2 tablespoons sugar and 2 tablespoons brandy or banana liqueur. Let the fruit macerate at least 2 hours. Add this mixture to the custard before freezing. Proceed with the recipe as directed.

CHOCOLATE FUDGE MALT ICE CREAM Add ½ cup chopped chocolate fudge (with or without nuts) to the machine when the ice cream is semifrozen. Allow the machine to mix in the candy. Proceed with the recipe as directed.

CHOCOLATE MALTED BALL ICE CREAM Add ½ cup chopped malted milk balls to the machine when the ice cream is semifrozen. Allow the machine to mix in the candy. Proceed with the recipe as directed.

CHOCOLATE PEANUT BUTTER MALT ICE CREAM Beat ¼ cup smooth peanut butter into the hot custard before straining. Proceed with the recipe as directed, adding ½ cup chopped peanut butter cup candies to the machine when the ice cream is semifrozen. Allow the machine to mix in the candy.

TEXAS CHOCOLATE MALT ICE CREAM Add ½ teaspoon ground cinnamon to the custard along with the malted milk powder. Proceed with the recipe as directed, adding ½ cup chopped toasted pecans (see page xvi) to the machine when the ice cream is semifrozen. Allow the machine to mix in the nuts.

CHOCOLATE TRUFFLE ICE CREAM

SCALDED cream and bittersweet chocolate make up the classic French mixture called *ganache*. Usually used for making truffles, ganache is the prefect base for extra-rich chocolate ice cream. Use the best quality chocolate you can find: the better the chocolate, the better the ice cream.

½ cup sugar

2 large egg yolks

1 cup milk

¼ cup cocoa powder

1½ cups heavy cream

6 ounces bittersweet
    chocolate, chopped

1 teaspoon vanilla extract

In a small mixing bowl, beat the sugar into the egg yolks until thickened and pale yellow. Set aside.

Bring the milk to a simmer in a heavy medium saucepan. Whisk in the cocoa and bring the milk back to a simmer. Simmer 3 minutes, stirring constantly. Slowly beat the hot milk and cocoa into the eggs and sugar. Pour the entire mixture back into the pan and place over low heat. Stir constantly with a whisk or wooden spoon until the custard thickens slightly. Be careful not to let the mixture boil or the eggs will scramble. Remove from the heat and pour the hot chocolate custard through a strainer into a large, clean bowl. Set aside while you prepare the ganache.

Bring the cream to a simmer in a small saucepan. Immediately remove from the heat and pour the cream over the chopped chocolate in a bowl. Stir until the chocolate is melted and the mixture is smooth. Combine the chocolate mixtures, then stir in the vanilla. Cover and refrigerate until cold or overnight.

Stir the chilled custard, then freeze in 1 or 2 batches in your ice cream machine according to the manufacturer's instructions. When finished, the ice cream will be soft but ready to eat. For firmer ice cream, transfer to a freezer-safe container and freeze at least 2 hours.

Variations

CHOCOLATE CABERNET CRUNCH ICE CREAM Bring 2 cups red wine (cabernet sauvignon) to a boil in a small, heavy saucepan. Boil until the wine is reduced to about ½ cup and is thick and slightly syrupy, about 10 minutes. Let this syrup cool, then stir into the custard before freezing. Proceed with the recipe as directed, adding ½ cup crumbled biscotti to the machine when the ice cream is semifrozen. Allow the machine to mix in the biscotti.

CHOCOLATE RASPBERRY ICE CREAM Stir 2 tablespoons water into ½ cup raspberry jam to loosen it up. Swirl the jam into the finished ice cream. Take care not to overswirl or the jam will "melt" into the ice cream. Streaks of jam should be visible. Serve immediately or freeze until firm.

KENTUCKY CHOCOLATE ICE CREAM Add ½ teaspoon peppermint extract and ¼ cup bourbon before freezing. Proceed with the recipe as directed.

ORANGETTE ICE CREAM Add 1 teaspoon orange extract along with the vanilla. Proceed with the recipe as directed. Swirl ½ cup chocolate syrup or chocolate sauce into the finished ice cream. Take care not to overswirl, or the chocolate will "melt" into the ice cream. Streaks of chocolate should be visible. Serve immediately or freeze until firm.

CHOCOLATE YOGURT ICE CREAM

FOR best results, use the mildest-tasting yogurt you can find.

1½ cups plain yogurt

1¼ cups sugar

1½ cups light cream

4 ounces unsweetened
   baking chocolate

1 teaspoon vanilla extract

Soak a large piece of cheesecloth or plain white paper towel in cold water. Squeeze out the water and line a colander or sieve with the wet cloth. Spoon the yogurt into the colander and set it into a larger bowl to catch the liquid that drains from the yogurt. Place in the refrigerator and let drain for 2 or 3 hours. Approximately ½ cup of liquid will drain out.

Meanwhile, combine the sugar, cream, and chocolate in a heavy medium saucepan. Set over low heat until the sugar is dissolved and the chocolate is completely melted. Remove from the heat and cool slightly. Stir in the thickened yogurt and the vanilla. Cover and refrigerate until cold or overnight.

Stir the chilled mixture, then freeze in 1 or 2 batches in your ice cream machine according to the manufacturer's instructions. When finished, the ice cream will be soft but ready to eat. For firmer ice cream, transfer to a freezer-safe container and freeze at least 2 hours.

◄ • ►

Variations

CHOCOLATE CRANBERRY YOGURT ICE CREAM Add ½ cup dried cranberries to the machine when the ice cream is semifrozen. Allow the machine to mix in the cranberries. Proceed with the recipe as directed.

DARK CHOCOLATE MINT YOGURT ICE CREAM Substitute 1 teaspoon peppermint extract for the vanilla extract. Proceed with the recipe as directed. Optional: add ¼ cup crumbled chocolate-covered mint candies to the machine when the ice cream is semifrozen.

MOCHACCINO YOGURT ICE CREAM Add 1 teaspoon instant espresso powder to the pan along with the cream. Proceed with the recipe as directed.

CINNAMON ICE CREAM

ALTHOUGH cinnamon is one of the most common spices, not all varieties of cinnamon are created equal. Cinnamon varies in taste and intensity, depending on how old it is and where it was grown. This recipe calls for 1 teaspoon of ground cinnamon, but you can adjust it up or down to suit your own taste and the strength of the cinnamon you have on hand. I prefer Vietnamese cinnamon, available from Penzeys in Muskego, Wisconsin (414-574-0277).

⅔ cup sugar

2 large egg yolks

1 tablespoon cornstarch

1 teaspoon ground
cinnamon

1 bay leaf

1½ cups milk

1½ cups light cream

In a medium mixing bowl, beat the sugar into the eggs until thickened and pale yellow. Beat in the cornstarch. Set aside.

Combine the cinnamon, bay leaf, and milk in a heavy medium saucepan. Bring to a simmer over low heat. Turn off the heat, cover, and let steep for 10 minutes. Remove the bay leaf and slowly beat the hot milk into the eggs and sugar. Pour the entire mixture back into the pan and place over low heat. Stir constantly with a whisk or wooden spoon until the custard thickens slightly. Be careful not to let the mixture boil or the eggs will scramble. Remove from the heat and pour the warm cinnamon custard through a strainer into a large, clean bowl. Allow the custard to cool slightly, then stir in the cream. Cover and refrigerate until cold or overnight.

Stir the chilled custard, then freeze in 1 or 2 batches in your ice cream machine according to the manufacturer's instructions. When finished, the ice cream will be soft but ready to eat. For firmer ice cream, transfer to a freezer-safe container and freeze at least 2 hours.

◂ • ▸

Variations

CINNAMON CHOCOLATE CHIP ICE CREAM
Add ½ cup miniature chocolate chips to the machine when the ice cream is semifrozen. Allow the machine to mix in the chips. Proceed with the recipe as directed.

continued

CINNAMON HARVEST ICE CREAM Add 1 cup granola with raisins and ¼ teaspoon ground nutmeg to the machine when the ice cream is semifrozen. Allow the machine to mix in the additional ingredients. Proceed with the recipe as directed.

CINNAMON SNICKERDOODLE ICE CREAM Add ½ teaspoon ground nutmeg and 1 cup crumbled chocolate chip cookies or 1 cup crumbled snickerdoodles, if you can find them, to the machine when the ice cream is semifrozen. Allow the machine to mix in the additional ingredients. Proceed with the recipe as directed.

CINNAMON ICE CREAM, PHILADELPHIA STYLE

MAKES JUST UNDER 1 QUART

THIS version of cinnamon ice cream is very easy to make and has a strong, pure, cinnamon flavor.

3 cups light cream

⅔ cup sugar

¼ teaspoon vanilla extract

1 teaspoon ground
    cinnamon

Heat the cream in a large, heavy saucepan over medium heat until small bubbles appear around the edge. Do not let the cream boil. Remove from the heat, add the sugar, and stir until it is completely dissolved. Whisk in the vanilla and cinnamon. Cool to room temperature. Cover and refrigerate until cold or overnight. The cinnamon will rise to the top, but don't worry: it will incorporate into the ice cream while it freezes.

Stir the chilled custard, then freeze in 1 or 2 batches in your ice cream machine according to the manufacturer's instructions. When finished, the ice cream will be soft but ready to eat. For firmer ice cream, transfer to a freezer-safe container and freeze at least 2 hours.

‹ • ›

Variations

CINNAMON BASIL ICE CREAM Finely mince 6 fresh basil leaves and add them to the cream before heating. Proceed with the recipe as directed.

CINNAMON BURST ICE CREAM Add ½ cup red-hot candies to the machine when the ice cream is semifrozen. Allow the machine to mix in the candy. Proceed with the recipe as directed.

CINNAMON BUTTERSCOTCH ICE CREAM Swirl ½ cup butterscotch sauce into the finished ice cream. Take care not to overswirl or the sauce will "melt" into the ice cream. Streaks of butterscotch should be visible. Serve immediately or freeze until firm.

NOUVEAU CINNAMON ICE CREAM Add ½ teaspoon ground black pepper and 1 cup crushed strawberries to the warm cream. Proceed with the recipe as directed.

COCONUT ICE CREAM

MAKES ABOUT 6 CUPS

L ACED with the chewiness of toasted, shredded coconut, this ice cream is wonderful on its own or spread in a cooked pie shell and covered in meringue, then browned quickly under the broiler for a Baked Alaska Coconut Pie.

½ cup shredded sweetened
  coconut
1 cup sugar
3 large eggs
1 teaspoon cornstarch
¼ teaspoon salt
1 cup half-and-half
1½ cups unsweetened
  coconut milk
1 cup heavy cream
2 teaspoons vanilla extract

Preheat the oven to 400°F. Spread the coconut on a baking sheet lined with aluminum foil. Place in the hot oven for 5 to 7 minutes, or until the coconut turns a light brown. Remove from the oven and allow to cool.

In a medium mixing bowl, beat the sugar into the eggs until thickened and pale yellow. Beat in the cornstarch and salt. Set aside.

Combine the half-and-half with the coconut milk in a heavy medium saucepan. Bring to a boil over medium heat. Remove from the heat and slowly beat the hot liquid into the eggs and sugar. Pour the entire mixture back into the pan and place over low heat. Stir constantly with a whisk or wooden spoon until the custard thickens slightly. Be careful not to let the mixture boil or the eggs will scramble. Remove from the heat and pour the hot custard through a strainer into a large, clean bowl. Allow the custard to cool slightly, then stir in the toasted coconut, cream, and vanilla. Cover and refrigerate until cold or overnight.

Stir the chilled custard, then freeze in 1 or 2 batches in your ice cream machine according to the manufacturer's instructions. When finished, the ice cream will be soft but ready to eat. For firmer ice cream, transfer to a freezer-safe container and freeze at least 2 hours.

Variations

COCONUT CHOCOLATE ICE CREAM Add 4 ounces melted semisweet chocolate to the warm custard before adding the cream. Proceed with the recipe as directed.

COCONUT CREAM PIE ICE CREAM Add ½ cup crumbled graham crackers to the machine when the ice cream is semifrozen. Allow the machine to mix in the crackers. Proceed with the recipe as directed.

COCONUT DREAM PIE ICE CREAM Add ½ cup drained crushed pineapple and ½ cup crumbled graham crackers to the machine when the ice cream is semifrozen. Allow the machine to mix in the additional ingredients. Proceed with the recipe as directed.

COCONUT SUNSHINE ICE CREAM Add ¼ cup orange liqueur before freezing. Proceed with the recipe as directed.

TROPIC DELIGHT ICE CREAM Add ¼ cup dark rum before freezing. Proceed with the recipe as directed.

COFFEE ICE CREAM

DIFFERENT varieties of coffee beans will impart different flavors to this ice cream, so choose your favorite, including decaffeinated beans.

¾ cup sugar

3 large egg yolks

2 teaspoons all-purpose
  flour

¼ teaspoon salt

1 cup milk

¾ cup whole coffee beans

1½ cups heavy cream

½ teaspoon vanilla extract

In a medium mixing bowl, beat the sugar into the egg yolks until they are thickened and pale yellow. Beat in the flour and salt. Set aside.

Combine the milk and coffee beans in a heavy medium saucepan. Bring to a boil over medium heat. Lower the heat, cover, and keep warm for 20 minutes.

Remove the coffee beans with a skimmer or slotted spoon. Slowly beat the warm milk into the eggs and sugar. Pour the entire mixture back into the pan and place over low heat. Stir constantly with a whisk or wooden spoon until the custard thickens slightly. Be careful not to let the mixture boil or the eggs will scramble. Remove from the heat and pour the hot coffee custard through a strainer into a large, clean bowl. Allow the custard to cool slightly, then stir in the cream and vanilla. Cover and refrigerate until cold or overnight.

Stir the chilled custard, then freeze in 1 or 2 batches in your ice cream machine according to the manufacturer's instructions. When finished, the ice cream will be soft but ready to eat. For firmer ice cream, transfer to a freezer-safe container and freeze at least 2 hours.

Variations

COFFEE CAKE ICE CREAM Add ½ teaspoon ground cinnamon along with the coffee beans. Proceed with the recipe as directed, adding ½ cup crumbled coffee cake to the machine when the ice cream is semifrozen. Allow the machine to mix in the cake.

COFFEE NUT ICE CREAM Add ½ cup chopped toasted pecans (see page xvi) to the machine when the ice cream is semifrozen. Allow the machine to mix in the nuts. Proceed with the recipe as directed.

COFFEE RASPBERRY ICE CREAM Stir 2 tablespoons water into ½ cup raspberry jam to loosen it up. Swirl the jam into the finished ice cream. Take care not to overswirl or the jam will "melt" into the ice cream. Streaks of jam should be visible. Serve immediately or freeze until firm.

FLAVORED COFFEE BEAN ICE CREAM Substitute your favorite flavored coffee beans, such as vanilla almond, hazelnut, or Irish cream, for regular coffee beans. Proceed with the recipe as directed.

IRISH COFFEE ICE CREAM Mix in ¼ cup whiskey before freezing. Proceed with the recipe as directed.

COFFEE ICE CREAM, PHILADELPHIA STYLE

MAKES ABOUT 1 QUART

THE high fat content of cream requires a longer steeping time to infuse the coffee flavor from the beans. Let the mixture sit overnight in the refrigerator for a very strong and rich coffee flavor.

3½ cups heavy cream

¾ cup sugar

1 cup whole coffee beans

Heat the cream in a large heavy saucepan over medium heat until small bubbles appear around the edge. Do not let the cream boil. Remove from the heat and add the sugar. Stir until the sugar dissolves completely. Stir in the coffee beans. Cover and cool to room temperature, then refrigerate overnight.

Strain out the coffee beans. Freeze in 1 or 2 batches in your ice cream machine according to the manufacturer's instructions. When finished, the ice cream will be soft but ready to eat. For firmer ice cream, transfer to a freezer-safe container and freeze at least 2 hours.

◄ • ►

Variations

COFFEE CORDIAL ICE CREAM Add ¼ cup coffee liqueur to the cream along with the sugar. Proceed with the recipe as directed.

MEXICAN COFFEE ICE CREAM Add ½ teaspoon ground cinnamon along with the coffee beans. Proceed with the recipe as directed.

CORN ICE CREAM

As delicious as it is unusual, this ice cream is great served on its own or on top of a warm slice of Sweet Cornbread Cake (recipe follows).

¾ cup sugar

4 large egg yolks

½ cup maple syrup

1 cup half-and-half

1½ cups canned cream-
  style corn

1 cup heavy cream

1 teaspoon vanilla extract

In a medium mixing bowl, beat the sugar into the egg yolks until thickened and pale yellow. Beat in the maple syrup. Set aside.

Bring the half-and-half to a simmer in a large, heavy saucepan. Slowly beat the hot half-and-half into the eggs and sugar. Pour the entire mixture back into the pan and place over low heat. Stir constantly with a whisk or wooden spoon until the custard thickens slightly. Be careful not to let the mixture boil or the eggs will scramble.

Remove from the heat and mix in the creamed corn. Pass the puree through a food mill to remove the skins. You may use a strainer, but the puree will be thick and will need to be "rubbed" through, using a large wooden spoon. If a chunky ice cream is desired, simply allow the custard to cool slightly, without straining.

Stir in the cream and vanilla. Cover and refrigerate until cold or overnight.

Stir the chilled custard, then freeze in 1 or 2 batches in your ice cream machine according to the manufacturer's instructions. When finished, the ice cream will be soft but ready to eat. For firmer ice cream, transfer to a freezer-safe container and freeze at least 2 hours.

◂ • ▸

Variations

CORN PUDDING ICE CREAM Add ¾ cup mini-marshmallows to the machine when the ice cream is semifrozen. Allow the machine to mix in the candy. Proceed with the recipe as directed.

continued

INDIAN SUMMER ICE CREAM Add ¼ cup raisins, ¼ cup unsalted sunflower seeds, and ¼ teaspoon ground nutmeg to the machine when the ice cream is semifrozen. Allow the machine to mix in the additional ingredients. Proceed with the recipe as directed.

SOUTHWESTERN ICE CREAM Add ½ teaspoon crushed red pepper flakes to the machine when the ice cream is semifrozen. Allow the machine to mix in the flakes. Proceed with the recipe as directed.

SUMMER SAVORY ICE CREAM Reduce the sugar to ½ cup. Add 1 teaspoon chopped fresh thyme and 1 teaspoon chopped fresh summer savory to the warm custard before adding the cream. Proceed with the recipe as directed.

SWEET CORNBREAD CAKE

MAKES 6 TO 8 SERVINGS

Tᴴɪs cake is sweeter than regular cornbread, making it the perfect dessert partner for Corn Ice Cream.

1 cup yellow cornmeal

1½ cups all-purpose flour

¾ cup sugar

1 tablespoon baking
  powder

½ teaspoon salt

2 cups buttermilk

2 large eggs, lightly beaten

¼ cup shortening or
  margarine, melted and
  cooled

Preheat the oven to 400°F. Grease a 9-inch square baking pan and set aside.

In a large mixing bowl, combine the cornmeal, flour, sugar, baking powder, and salt. Stir until well mixed. Add the buttermilk, eggs, and shortening. Mix until smooth, about 1 minute.

Pour the batter into the prepared pan and bake until lightly browned, 25 to 30 minutes, or until a toothpick inserted into the center comes out clean.

EARL GREY ICE CREAM

FOR the ultimate frozen iced tea treat, try this ice cream alongside a scoop of lemon sorbet.

1 cup milk

3 heaping tablespoons loose Earl Grey tea or 5 to 6 Earl Grey tea bags

¾ cup sugar

6 large egg yolks

2 teaspoons all-purpose flour

¼ teaspoon salt

1 cup half-and-half

1 cup heavy cream

Bring the milk to a boil in a heavy medium saucepan. Remove from the heat. Stir in the tea leaves or bags, cover, and set aside to steep for 15 minutes.

Meanwhile, in a medium mixing bowl, beat the sugar into the egg yolks until thickened and pale yellow. Beat in the flour and salt. Set aside.

Strain the milk to remove the tea leaves, or simply remove the tea bags. Add the half-and-half and return to a simmer over low heat. Slowly beat the hot milk and half-and-half into the egg yolks and sugar. Pour the entire mixture back into the pan and place over low heat. Stir constantly with a whisk or wooden spoon until the custard thickens slightly. Be careful not to let the mixture boil or the eggs will scramble. Remove from the heat and pour the hot tea custard through a strainer into a large, clean bowl. Allow the custard to cool slightly, then stir in the cream. Cover and refrigerate until cold or overnight.

Stir the chilled custard, then freeze in 1 or 2 batches in your ice cream machine according to the manufacturer's instructions. When finished, the ice cream will be soft but ready to eat. For firmer ice cream, transfer to a freezer-safe container and freeze at least 2 hours.

◄ • ▸

Variations

DEVONSHIRE ICE CREAM Add 2 teaspoons vanilla before freezing. Proceed with the recipe as directed.

continued

EARL GREY AND DRIED FRUITS ICE CREAM Cover ¼ cup dried currants and ¼ cup chopped dried apricots with boiling water and let sit for 1 hour, or until soft. Drain the fruit and add to the machine when ice cream is semifrozen. Allow the machine to mix in the fruit. Proceed with the recipe as directed.

ENGLISH SUMMER ICE CREAM Stir in ½ cup crushed fresh strawberries, ¼ cup currants, and 1 teaspoon freshly grated lemon zest before freezing. Proceed with the recipe as directed.

TEA AND SYMPATHY ICE CREAM Add 1 cup crumbled scones to the machine when the ice cream is semifrozen. Allow the machine to mix in the scones. Proceed with the recipe as directed.

FIG ICE CREAM

DRIED figs have a more intense flavor than fresh figs, making them perfect for ice cream. Look for ones that are semimoist, not hard or desiccated.

8 dried figs

2 large eggs

1½ cups milk

½ cup sugar

1 cup heavy cream

½ teaspoon vanilla extract

¼ teaspoon salt

Cover the dried figs with boiling water and set aside until soft, about 2 hours. Drain the figs, cut into quarters, and place in a food processor. Add the eggs and process until smooth, about 1 minute.

Combine the milk and sugar in a medium saucepan and place over low heat. Stir until the sugar dissolves and the milk comes to a boil. Immediately remove from the heat. With the food processor running, slowly pour the hot milk into the fig mixture through the feed tube. Process until completely smooth. Pour the mixture into a large, clean bowl and allow to cool slightly. Stir in the cream, vanilla, and salt. Cover and refrigerate until cold or overnight.

Stir the chilled custard, then freeze in 1 or 2 batches in your ice cream machine according to the manufacturer's instructions. When finished, the ice cream will be soft but ready to eat. For firmer ice cream, transfer to a freezer-safe container and freeze at least 2 hours.

Variations

FIG ALMOND ICE CREAM Add ¼ teaspoon almond extract along with the vanilla extract. Add ½ cup chopped toasted almonds (see page xvi) to the machine when the ice cream is semifrozen. Allow the machine to mix in the nuts. Proceed with the recipe as directed.

FIG COOKIE ICE CREAM Add ½ cup crumbled sugar cookies to the machine when the ice cream is semifrozen. Allow the machine to mix in the cookies. Proceed with the recipe as directed.

continued

FIG TART ICE CREAM Substitute honey for sugar. Add 1 teaspoon grated fresh orange zest and 3 crumbled graham crackers to the machine when the ice cream is semifrozen. Allow the machine to mix in the additional ingredients. Proceed with the recipe as directed.

PROMISED LAND ICE CREAM Add ¼ cup chopped dried dates, ¼ cup raisins, and ½ cup crumbled mandelbrot or other dry cake to the machine when the ice cream is semifrozen. Allow the machine to mix in the additional ingredients. Proceed with the recipe as directed.

SPICED FIGGIE PUDDING ICE CREAM Add ½ teaspoon ground cinnamon, ¼ teaspoon ground nutmeg, and ⅛ teaspoon ground mace to the milk along with the sugar. Proceed with the recipe as directed.

GINGER ICE CREAM

MAKES ABOUT 1 QUART

THIS recipe calls for fresh as well as crystallized ginger, which can both be found in many supermarkets or by mail from Whole Foods (800-780-3663). Powdered ginger will not work in this recipe.

¾ cup sugar

3 large eggs

2 teaspoons cornstarch

One 4-inch piece fresh
  ginger, peeled

1 cup milk

1½ cups heavy cream

½ teaspoon vanilla extract

2 tablespoons finely
  chopped crystallized
  ginger

In a mixing bowl, beat the sugar into the eggs until thickened and pale yellow. Beat in the cornstarch. Set aside.

Slice the ginger into ½-inch pieces and combine with the milk in a heavy medium saucepan. Bring to a boil, then remove from the heat, cover, and let steep for 15 minutes. Remove the ginger with a slotted spoon and slowly beat the warm milk into the eggs and sugar. Pour the entire mixture back into the pan and place over low heat. Stir constantly with a whisk or wooden spoon until the custard thickens slightly. Be careful not to let the mixture boil or the eggs will scramble. Remove from the heat and pour the hot ginger custard through a strainer into a large, clean bowl. Allow the custard to cool slightly, then stir in the cream and vanilla. Cover and refrigerate until cold or overnight.

Stir the chilled custard, then freeze in 1 or 2 batches in your ice cream machine according to the manufacturer's instructions, adding the crystallized ginger to the machine when the ice cream is semifrozen. When finished, the ice cream will be soft but ready to eat. For firmer ice cream, transfer to a freezer-safe container and freeze at least 2 hours.

◄ • ►

Variations

EAST INDIA TRADING COMPANY ICE CREAM
Along with the ginger, add to the milk ¼ teaspoon each of the following: ground cinnamon, ground nutmeg, ground cardamom. Proceed with the recipe as directed.

continued

GINGER COOKIE ICE CREAM Add ½ cup crumbled ginger snaps to the machine when the ice cream is semifrozen. Allow the machine to mix in the cookies. Proceed with the recipe as directed.

GINGER NUT ICE CREAM Add ½ cup chopped toasted walnuts (see page xvi) to the machine when the ice cream is semifrozen. Allow the machine to mix in the nuts. Proceed with the recipe as directed.

GINGER TEA ICE CREAM Add 2 tea bags of black tea to steep in the milk along with the ginger. Remove the tea bags with the ginger. Proceed with the recipe as directed.

GINGER VERBENA ICE CREAM Add 6 leaves fresh lemon verbena to steep in the milk along with the ginger. Strain the leaves out with the ginger. Proceed with the recipe as directed.

PFEFFERNUSS ICE CREAM Add ½ teaspoon ground cinnamon and ¼ teaspoon ground nutmeg to the milk along with the ginger. Add ½ cup crumbled sugar cookies to the machine when the ice cream is semifrozen. Allow the machine to mix in the cookies. Proceed with the recipe as directed.

GREEN TEA ICE CREAM

MAKES ABOUT 3 CUPS

I FIND that loose tea leaves work better in this recipe than green tea in bags. Also, green tea can vary in strength depending on the brand; for this recipe, the stronger, the better.

> 2 cups milk
>
> 3 tablespoons green tea leaves
>
> ⅔ cup sugar
>
> 2 large egg yolks
>
> 1 tablespoon cornstarch
>
> 1 cup heavy cream

Bring the milk to a boil in a heavy medium saucepan. Remove from the heat. Stir in the tea leaves, cover, and set aside to steep for 10 to 15 minutes.

Meanwhile, in a medium mixing bowl, beat the sugar into the egg yolks until thickened and pale yellow. Beat in the cornstarch.

Strain the milk to remove the tea leaves and slowly beat the warm milk into the egg yolks and sugar. Pour the entire mixture back into the pan and place over low heat. Stir constantly with a whisk or wooden spoon until the custard thickens slightly. Be careful not to let the mixture boil or the eggs will scramble. Remove from the heat and pour the hot tea custard through a strainer into a large, clean bowl. Allow the custard to cool slightly, then stir in the cream. Cover and refrigerate until cold or overnight.

Stir the chilled custard, then freeze in 1 or 2 batches in your ice cream machine according to the manufacturer's instructions. When finished, the ice cream will be soft but ready to eat. For firmer ice cream, transfer to a freezer-safe container and freeze at least 2 hours.

◄ • ►

Variations

ASIA SPICE ICE CREAM Add ½ teaspoon crushed Szechwan peppercorns to the warm custard along with the cream. Proceed with the recipe as directed.

continued

GREEN FORTUNE ICE CREAM Add ½ cup crumbled fortune cookies to the machine when the ice cream is semifrozen. Allow the machine to mix in the cookies. Proceed with the recipe as directed.

SWEET AND SOUR ICE CREAM Add the grated zest of 1 lemon to the warm custard along with the cream. Proceed with the recipe as directed.

HAZELNUT ICE CREAM

MAKES ABOUT 1 QUART

HAZELNUTS are also called filberts. Buy them roasted and unsalted.

1 cup roasted unsalted
   hazelnuts
¼ cup hazelnut syrup or
   liqueur
4 large egg yolks
1 teaspoon all-purpose
   flour
1½ cups milk
½ cup sugar
1 cup heavy cream

Remove any skins from the nuts by rubbing a handful together between the palms of your hands. The skins will slip off. Repeat the process until all the nuts are cleaned. Place the nuts and syrup in a food processor and process for 2 minutes or until the nuts are completely smooth. Add the egg yolks and process until well blended, about 30 seconds. Add the flour and process 10 seconds more.

Combine the milk and sugar in a heavy medium saucepan. Place over medium heat and stir until the sugar dissolves and the milk comes to a boil. Immediately remove from the heat. With the food processor running, slowly pour the hot milk into the nut puree through the feed tube. Process 30 seconds or until the nut custard is smooth. Pour the entire mixture back into the pan and place over low heat. Stir until the mixture thickens slightly, being careful not to let the mixture boil or the eggs will scramble. Pour the hot hazelnut custard through a strainer to remove any bits of unground nut or skin. Allow the custard to cool slightly, then stir in the cream. Cover and refrigerate until cold or overnight.

Stir the chilled custard, then freeze in 1 or 2 batches in your ice cream machine according to the manufacturer's instructions. When finished, the ice cream will be soft but ready to eat. For firmer ice cream, transfer to a freezer-safe container and freeze at least 2 hours.

◄ • ►

Variations

HAZELNUT CINNAMON ICE CREAM
Add ½ teaspoon ground cinnamon to the food processor along with the nuts. Proceed with the recipe as directed, adding 1 teaspoon vanilla extract along with the cream.

continued

HAZELNUT CRUNCH ICE CREAM Add ½ cup toasted hazelnut halves (see page xvi) to the machine when the ice cream is semifrozen. Allow the machine to mix in the nuts. Proceed with the recipe as directed.

HAZELNUT TART ICE CREAM Substitute honey for the hazelnut syrup or liqueur. Proceed with the recipe as directed, adding 4 crumbled graham crackers to the machine when the ice cream is semifrozen. Allow the machine to mix in the crackers.

HONEY ICE CREAM

MAKES ABOUT 1 QUART

USE a light-colored honey for this ice cream: perhaps clover, orange blossom, rhododendron, heather, or wildflower. Darker honeys such as chestnut, pine, and rosemary are too strong and can easily overpower this delicate dessert.

½ cup mild honey

6 large egg yolks

1½ cups milk

1 cup heavy cream

1 teaspoon vanilla extract

In a medium mixing bowl, beat the honey with the egg yolks until thickened and pale yellow. Set aside.

Bring the milk to a simmer in a heavy medium saucepan. Slowly beat the hot milk into the eggs and honey. Pour the entire mixture back into the pan and place over low heat. Stir constantly with a whisk or wooden spoon until the custard thickens slightly. Be careful not to let the mixture boil or the eggs will scramble. Remove from the heat and pour the hot honey custard through a strainer into a large, clean bowl. Allow the custard to cool slightly, then stir in the cream and vanilla. Cover and refrigerate until cold or overnight.

Stir the chilled custard, then freeze in 1 or 2 batches in your ice cream machine according to the manufacturer's instructions. When finished, the ice cream will be soft but ready to eat. For firmer ice cream, transfer to a freezer-safe container and freeze at least 2 hours.

◂ • ▸

Variations

HONEY CORDIAL ICE CREAM Add ¼ cup honey liqueur before freezing. Proceed with the recipe as directed.

HONEY CRUNCH ICE CREAM Add 1 cup granola to the machine when the ice cream is semifrozen. Allow the machine to mix in the granola. Proceed with the recipe as directed.

continued

HONEY FLOWER ICE CREAM Add 2 teaspoons rose water or orange flower water to the milk before heating. Add ¼ cup candied rose petals or violets to the machine when the ice cream is semifrozen. Allow the machine to mix in the flowers. Proceed with the recipe as directed.

HONEY MARSHMALLOW ICE CREAM Swirl ½ cup marshmallow creme into finished ice cream. Take care not to overswirl or the sauce will "melt" into the ice cream. Streaks of marshmallow should be visible. Serve immediately or freeze until firm.

HONEY NUT ICE CREAM Add ½ cup chopped toasted pecans (see page xvi) to the machine when the ice cream is semifrozen. Allow the machine to mix in the nuts. Proceed with the recipe as directed.

MEAD ICE CREAM Add ¼ cup whiskey to the custard before freezing. Proceed with the recipe as directed.

IRISH ICE CREAM

MAKES ABOUT 3 CUPS

THIS recipe uses a large amount of Irish cream liqueur, a whiskey-based drink. It is boiled down to concentrate the flavor, so most of the alcohol is cooked away.

1½ cups Irish cream
  liqueur
½ cup sugar
3 large egg yolks
1 cup milk
1 cup heavy cream
1 teaspoon vanilla extract

Bring the liqueur to a simmer in a small, heavy saucepan placed over medium heat. Cook until the liqueur is reduced to about ½ cup, 5 to 7 minutes. The liqueur will appear thicker and slightly syrupy. Set aside.

In a medium mixing bowl, beat the sugar into the egg yolks until thickened and pale yellow. Set aside.

Bring the milk to a simmer in a heavy medium saucepan. Slowly beat the hot milk into the eggs and sugar. Pour the entire mixture back into the pan and place over low heat. Stir constantly with a whisk or wooden spoon until the custard thickens slightly. Be careful not to let the mixture boil or the eggs will scramble. Remove from the heat and pour the hot custard through a strainer into a large, clean bowl. Allow the custard to cool slightly. Mix in the reduced liqueur, cream, and vanilla. Cover and refrigerate until cold or overnight.

Stir the chilled custard, then freeze in 1 or 2 batches in your ice cream machine according to the manufacturer's instructions. When finished, the ice cream will be soft but ready to eat. For firmer ice cream, transfer to a freezer-safe container and freeze at least 2 hours.

◄ • ►

Variations

IRISH ALMOND ICE CREAM
Add ½ cup amaretto liqueur to the Irish cream liqueur before reducing. Add ¼ cup crumbled amaretti cookies to the machine when the ice cream is semifrozen. Allow the machine to mix in the cookies. Proceed with the recipe as directed.

continued

IRISH CHOCOLATE CHIP ICE CREAM Add ½ cup chocolate chips to the machine when the ice cream is semifrozen. Allow the machine to mix in the chocolate chips. Proceed with the recipe as directed.

IRISH COFFEE ICE CREAM Add 1 teaspoon instant espresso powder to the milk before heating. Proceed with the recipe as directed.

IRISH COUNTRY ICE CREAM Add 1 cup crushed fresh strawberries to the custard before freezing. Proceed with the recipe as directed.

IRISH PISTACHIO ICE CREAM Add ½ cup chopped unsalted pistachios to the machine when the ice cream is semifrozen. Allow the machine to mix in the nuts. Proceed with the recipe as directed.

KEY LIME ICE CREAM

I F you can't find fresh key limes or bottled key lime juice, you can use fresh-squeezed regular lime juice instead.

1½ cups heavy cream

6 large egg yolks

One 15-ounce can
   sweetened condensed
   milk

½ cup key lime juice (fresh
   from 8 to 10 medium
   limes or use bottled)

Bring the cream to a simmer in a heavy medium saucepan. Slowly beat the hot cream into the egg yolks in a medium mixing bowl. Pour the entire mixture back into the pan and place over low heat. Stir constantly with a whisk or wooden spoon until the custard thickens slightly. Be careful not to let the mixture boil or the eggs will scramble. Remove from the heat and pour the hot custard through a strainer into a large, clean bowl. Allow the custard to cool slightly, then stir in the sweetened condensed milk and key lime juice. Cover and refrigerate until cold or overnight.

Stir the cold custard well, then freeze in 1 or 2 batches in your ice cream machine according to the manufacturer's instructions. When finished, the ice cream will be soft but ready to eat. For firmer ice cream, transfer to a freezer-safe container and freeze at least 2 hours.

◄ • ►

Variations

DAIQUIRI ICE CREAM Add ½ cup gold rum before freezing. Proceed with the recipe as directed.

KEY LIME PIE ICE CREAM Add ½ cup mini-marshmallows and 4 crumbled graham crackers to the machine when the ice cream is semifrozen. Allow the machine to mix in the additional ingredients. Proceed with the recipe as directed.

MARGARITA ICE CREAM Add ¼ cup tequila and ¼ cup orange liqueur before freezing. Proceed with the recipe as directed.

LAVENDER ICE CREAM

MAKES ABOUT 1 QUART

DRIED lavender is available at many spice stores or from spice suppliers. Make sure to ask if the flowers are safe to eat—do not buy lavender intended for potpourri.

3 cups light cream

2 tablespoons dried
   lavender flowers

¾ cup sugar

4 large egg yolks

2 teaspoons all-purpose
   flour

1 teaspoon rose water
   (optional)

Combine the light cream and lavender flowers in a heavy medium saucepan. Bring to a simmer, then remove from the heat. Cover the pan and allow the lavender flowers to steep in the hot cream for 15 minutes.

In a medium mixing bowl, beat the sugar into the egg yolks until thickened and pale yellow. Beat in the flour and set aside.

Strain the cream to remove the lavender flowers. Slowly beat the warm cream into the egg yolks. Pour the entire mixture back into the pan and place over low heat. Stir constantly with a whisk or wooden spoon until the custard thickens slightly. Be careful not to let the mixture boil or the eggs will scramble. Remove from the heat and pour the hot lavender custard through a strainer into a large, clean bowl. Allow the custard to cool slightly, then stir in the rose water. Cover and refrigerate until cold or overnight.

Stir the chilled custard, then freeze in 1 or 2 batches in your ice cream machine according to the manufacturer's instructions. When finished, the ice cream will be soft but ready to eat. For firmer ice cream, transfer to a freezer-safe container and freeze at least 2 hours.

Variations

HONEY LAVENDER ICE CREAM Replace the sugar with ⅔ cup honey. Proceed with the recipe as directed.

LAVENDER PETAL ICE CREAM Add 2 tablespoons candied violet or rose petals to the machine when the ice cream is semifrozen. Allow the machine to mix in the flowers. Proceed with the recipe as directed.

LEMON ICE CREAM

A LITTLE lemon extract helps bring out a bright lemon flavor in this recipe. Look for it wherever you buy vanilla extract or spices.

2 large eggs

1 cup sugar

½ cup fresh lemon juice
   from 5 to 6 large lemons

2 tablespoons butter

1 teaspoon lemon extract

2 cups light cream

Combine the eggs, sugar, lemon juice, and butter in the top of a double boiler. Place over simmering water and beat constantly until the mixture thickens, about 15 minutes. Allow the lemon curd to cool slightly. Stir in the lemon extract and cream. Cover and refrigerate until cold or overnight.

Stir the cold custard well, then freeze in 1 or 2 batches in your ice cream machine according to the manufacturer's instructions. When finished, the ice cream will be soft but ready to eat. For firmer ice cream, transfer to a freezer-safe container and freeze at least 2 hours.

‹ • ›

Variations

LEMON BOURBON ICE CREAM Add ¼ cup bourbon to the custard before freezing. Proceed with the recipe as directed. Optional: swirl ½ cup chocolate syrup or chocolate sauce into the finished ice cream. Take care not to overswirl or the sauce will "melt" into the ice cream. Streaks of chocolate should be visible. Serve immediately or freeze until firm.

LEMON MERINGUE PIE ICE CREAM Add ½ cup mini-marshmallows and ½ cup crumbled graham crackers to the machine when the ice cream is semifrozen. Allow the machine to mix in the additional ingredients. Proceed with the recipe as directed.

LEMON MINT ICE CREAM Mix 2 tablespoons finely minced fresh mint leaves into the custard along with the cream. Proceed with the recipe as directed.

LEMON POPPY SEED ICE CREAM Mix 1 tablespoon poppy seeds into the custard along with the cream. Proceed with the recipe as directed.

LEMON STRAWBERRY ICE CREAM Thinly slice 1 pint strawberries. Toss with 2 tablespoons sugar and let the fruit macerate at least 2 hours. Combine this mixture with the custard before freezing.

LEMON YOGURT ICE CREAM

LEMON is one flavor that complements the natural sourness of yogurt. Candied lemon zest helps add a touch of sweetness and texture to this very rich dessert.

One 32-ounce container
  plain yogurt
¾ cup sugar
½ cup fresh lemon juice
  from 5 to 6 large lemons
¼ cup candied lemon zest
  (recipe follows)
1 cup light cream

Soak a large piece of cheesecloth or plain white paper towel in cold water. Squeeze out the water and line a colander or sieve with the wet cloth. Spoon the yogurt into the colander and set it into a larger bowl to catch the liquid that drains from the yogurt. Place in the refrigerator and let drain for 2 to 3 hours. Approximately 1½ cups of liquid will drain out.

Spoon the thickened yogurt into a large mixing bowl and whisk in the sugar, lemon juice, and lemon zest. Stir until the sugar is completely dissolved. Stir in the cream. Freeze in your ice cream machine according to the manufacturer's directions. When finished, the ice cream will be soft but ready to eat. For firmer ice cream, transfer to a freezer-safe container and freeze at least 2 hours.

‹ • ›

Variations

HONEY LEMON YOGURT ICE CREAM Substitute ½ cup honey for ½ cup of the sugar. Proceed with the recipe as directed.

LEMON YOGURT COCONUT ICE CREAM Add ½ cup toasted sweetened coconut (see page xvi) to the machine when the ice cream is semifrozen. Allow the machine to mix in the coconut. Proceed with the recipe as directed.

LEMON YOGURT COOKIE ICE CREAM Add 1 cup crumbled oatmeal cookies to the machine when the ice cream is semifrozen. Allow the machine to mix in the cookies. Proceed with the recipe as directed.

LEMON YOGURT DROP ICE CREAM Add ¼ cup crushed lemon drop candies to the machine when the ice cream is semifrozen. Allow the machine to mix in the candy. Proceed with the recipe as directed.

CANDIED LEMON ZEST

1 large lemon
½ cup sugar

Use a sharp paring knife to cut the zest off the lemon. Cut only the yellow part, leaving the bitter white pith behind. Slice the zest into very thin strips, then place in a small saucepan and cover with water. Bring to a boil and immediately remove from the heat. Drain and repeat the boiling process 3 times. This will help soften the zest and remove any bitterness.

Return the zest to the pan with ½ cup water and the sugar. Stir over low heat until the sugar is dissolved. Bring to a simmer and cook until the zest is translucent, about 5 minutes. Remove the zest with a slotted spoon and use immediately or allow to cool in the syrup, then refrigerate until ready to use. Candied lemon zest can be stored in its syrup in the refrigerator for 2 weeks.

MANGO ICE CREAM

HAITIAN mangoes, Mexican mangoes, Californian mangoes, Australian mangoes—any mango will do as long as it's ripe and sweet. Look for fruit that's firm, not hard, with a noticeably sweet fragrance.

2 large, ripe mangoes

2 tablespoons fresh lime
    juice from 2 medium
    limes

¼ cup light corn syrup

¼ teaspoon salt

¾ cup sugar

2 large egg yolks

1 tablespoon cornstarch

1 cup milk

1 cup heavy cream

Peel the mangoes and cut away as much flesh from the pits as you can. Combine the cut-up mangoes, lime juice, corn syrup, and salt in a food processor. Process until completely smooth, stopping the machine to scrape down the sides once or twice. Pour the puree through a strainer to remove any fibrous pieces of mango. You should have about 1¾ cups of smooth mango puree. Set aside.

In a medium mixing bowl, beat the sugar into the egg yolks until thickened and pale yellow. Beat in the cornstarch. Set aside.

Bring the milk to a simmer in a heavy medium saucepan. Slowly beat the hot milk into the eggs and sugar. Pour the entire mixture back into the pan and place over low heat. Stir constantly with a whisk or wooden spoon until the custard thickens slightly. Be careful not to let the mixture boil or the eggs will scramble. Remove from the heat and pour the hot custard through a strainer into a large, clean bowl. Allow the custard to cool slightly, then stir in the mango puree and cream. Cover and refrigerate until cold or overnight.

Stir the chilled custard, then freeze in 1 or 2 batches in your ice cream machine according to the manufacturer's instructions. When finished, the ice cream will be soft but ready to eat. For firmer ice cream, transfer to a freezer-safe container and freeze at least 2 hours.

Variations

MANGO GINGER ICE CREAM Add 2 tablespoons chopped fresh ginger to the food processor along with the mango. Proceed with the recipe as directed. Add ½ cup crumbled ginger snaps to the machine when the ice cream is semifrozen. Allow the machine to mix in the cookies.

MANGO HAZELNUT ICE CREAM Add ¼ cup hazelnut syrup or liqueur to the custard before freezing. Proceed with the recipe as directed, adding ½ cup chopped toasted hazelnuts (see page xvi) to the machine when the ice cream is semifrozen. Allow the machine to mix in the nuts.

TROPICAL MANGO ICE CREAM Add ¼ cup chopped dried pineapple, ¼ cup toasted sweetened coconut (see page xvi), and 1 teaspoon grated fresh lime zest to the machine when the ice cream is semifrozen. Allow the machine to mix in the additional ingredients. Proceed with the recipe as directed.

MAPLE ICE CREAM

MAPLE syrup comes in three grades: light amber, medium amber, and dark amber. The darker the color, the stronger the flavor. Use medium or dark amber for this ice cream. Do not substitute maple-flavored pancake syrup.

6 large egg yolks

1 cup pure maple syrup

2 teaspoons all-purpose
   flour

½ teaspoon salt

1 cup half-and-half

1½ cups light cream

½ teaspoon vanilla extract

In a medium mixing bowl, beat the egg yolks with the maple syrup, flour, and salt. Set aside.

Bring the half-and-half to a simmer in a heavy medium saucepan. Slowly beat the hot half-and-half into the eggs and maple syrup. Pour the entire mixture back into the pan and place over low heat. Stir constantly with a whisk or wooden spoon until the custard thickens slightly. Be careful not to let the mixture boil or the eggs will scramble. Remove from the heat and pour the hot maple custard through a strainer into a large, clean bowl. Allow the custard to cool slightly, then stir in the cream and vanilla. Cover and refrigerate until cold or overnight.

Stir the chilled custard, then freeze in 1 or 2 batches in your ice cream machine according to the manufacturer's instructions. When finished, the ice cream will be soft but ready to eat. For firmer ice cream, transfer to a freezer-safe container and freeze at least 2 hours.

◄ • ►

Variations

MAPLE BANANA NUT ICE CREAM Thinly slice 2 small bananas. Toss with 2 tablespoons sugar and allow the fruit to macerate at least 2 hours. Combine this mixture with the custard before freezing. Proceed with the recipe as directed, adding ¼ cup chopped toasted pecans (see page xvi) to the machine when the ice cream is semifrozen. Allow the machine to mix in the nuts.

MAPLE CANDY ICE CREAM Add 1 cup chopped Mary Jane candies to the machine when the ice cream is semifrozen. Allow the machine to mix in the candy. Proceed with the recipe as directed.

MAPLE WAFFLE ICE CREAM Add 1 cup crumbled, toasted waffles to the machine when the ice cream is semifrozen. Allow the machine to mix in the waffles. Proceed with the recipe as directed.

MAPLE WALNUT ICE CREAM Add ½ cup chopped walnuts and ½ cup mini-marshmallows to the machine when the ice cream is semifrozen. Allow the machine to mix in the additional ingredients. Proceed with the recipe as directed.

SPICED MAPLE CRUNCH ICE CREAM Add 1 cup Red Pepper–Pecan Praline Crunch (see page 25) to the machine when the ice cream is semifrozen. Allow the machine to mix in the praline. Proceed with the recipe as directed.

MARMALADE ICE CREAM

MAKES ABOUT 1 QUART

THIS is one of the easiest ice creams to make. It's also one of the creamiest and softest, even after resting in the freezer overnight, so don't try to eat this one in a cone.

1 1/4 cups orange
  marmalade

1/2 teaspoon vanilla extract

2 tablespoons orange
  liqueur or syrup

1 cup half-and-half

1 cup heavy cream

In a large mixing bowl, combine the marmalade, vanilla, and liqueur or syrup. Mix well. Stir in the half-and-half and cream. Freeze in your ice cream machine according to the manufacturer's instructions.

When finished, the ice cream will be very soft but ready to eat. Although this ice cream will not freeze hard, you can transfer to a freezer-safe container and freeze to firm up a little more.

◄ • ►

Variations

APRICOT JAM ICE CREAM Use apricot jam and apricot liqueur or strawberry syrup.

BLACKBERRY JAM ICE CREAM Use blackberry jam and blackberry liqueur or blackberry syrup.

BLUEBERRY JAM ICE CREAM Use blueberry jam and crème de cassis or black currant syrup.

CHERRY JAM ICE CREAM Use cherry jam and cherry liqueur or cherry syrup.

PEACH JAM ICE CREAM Use peach jam and peach schnapps or peach syrup.

PLUM JAM ICE CREAM Increase jam to 1½ cups; use plum jam and Armagnac or brandy.

STRAWBERRY JAM ICE CREAM Use strawberry jam and strawberry schnapps or strawberry syrup.

MINT ICE CREAM

THIS ice cream is delicious on its own or with dark chocolate chips, or thin chocolate slivers, or crunchy chocolate cookies, or creamy chocolate mint candies. Well, any chocolate mixed in is terrific.

¾ cup sugar

2 large eggs

1 tablespoon cornstarch

2 cups half-and-half

1 cup heavy cream

2 teaspoons peppermint
   extract

6 drops green food
   coloring (optional)

In a medium mixing bowl, beat the sugar into the eggs until thickened and pale yellow. Beat in the cornstarch and set aside.

Bring the half-and-half to a simmer in a heavy medium saucepan. Slowly beat the hot half-and-half into the eggs and sugar. Pour the entire mixture back into the pan and place over low heat. Stir constantly with a whisk or wooden spoon until the custard thickens slightly. Be careful not to let the mixture boil or the eggs will scramble. Remove from the heat and pour the hot custard through a strainer into a large, clean bowl. Allow the custard to cool slightly, then stir in the cream, peppermint extract, and food coloring, if using. Cover and refrigerate until cold or overnight.

Stir the chilled custard, then freeze in 1 or 2 batches in your ice cream machine according to the manufacturer's instructions. When finished, the ice cream will be soft but ready to eat. For firmer ice cream, transfer to a freezer-safe container and freeze at least 2 hours.

◂ • ▸

Variations

AFTER-DINNER MINT ICE CREAM Add ¾ cup chopped chocolate-covered mint candies to the machine when the ice cream is semifrozen. Allow the machine to mix in the candy. Proceed with the recipe as directed.

GRASSHOPPER PIE ICE CREAM Add ½ cup white crème de cacao to the custard before freezing. Proceed with the recipe as directed, adding ½ cup crushed chocolate wafers to the machine when the ice cream is semifrozen. Allow the machine to mix in the wafers.

continued

ISLAND MINT ICE CREAM Add ½ cup gold rum to the custard before freezing. Proceed with the recipe as directed, adding ½ cup shredded, sweetened coconut to the machine when the ice cream is semifrozen. Allow the machine to mix in the coconut.

MINT-OREO CHEESECAKE ICE CREAM Add ½ cup no-bake cheesecake mix to the half-and-half before heating. Proceed with the recipe as directed, adding ½ cup crushed chocolate creme cookies to the machine when the ice cream is semifrozen. Allow the machine to mix in the cookies.

PEPPERMINT CANDY CRUNCH ICE CREAM Add ¾ cup crushed peppermint candies to the machine when the ice cream is semifrozen. Allow the machine to mix in the candy. Proceed with the recipe as directed.

MINT ICE CREAM, PHILADELPHIA STYLE

EASY to make and very delicious.

3 cups heavy cream

½ cup sugar

1 tablespoon peppermint
extract

Heat the cream in a heavy medium saucepan until small bubbles appear around the edge. Do not let the cream boil. Remove from the heat and add the sugar. Stir until the sugar dissolves completely. Cool to room temperature. Stir in the mint extract. Refrigerate until cold or overnight. Freeze in 1 or 2 batches in your ice cream machine according to the manufacturer's instructions.

When finished, the ice cream will be soft but ready to eat. For firmer ice cream, transfer to a freezer-safe container and freeze at least 2 hours.

◄ • ►

Variations

CLASSIC MINT CHIP ICE CREAM Add ¾ cup miniature chocolate chips to the machine when the ice cream is semifrozen. Allow the machine to mix in the candy. Proceed with the recipe as directed.

SPEARMINT ICE CREAM Substitute spearmint extract for peppermint extract. Proceed with the recipe as directed.

NOUGAT ICE CREAM

THIS ice cream doesn't require an ice cream machine. Simply pack it into a freezer-proof container and set in the freezer overnight to harden.

2 large egg whites

⅓ cup honey

½ cup sugar

¼ cup water

1½ cups heavy cream

½ teaspoon almond extract

½ cup chopped toasted almonds (see page xvi)

Beat the egg whites until soft peaks form. Combine the honey, sugar, and water in a small, heavy saucepan. Stir over low heat until the sugar dissolves and the syrup is clear. Raise the heat and bring the syrup to a boil. Boil without stirring for 2 minutes. Remove from the heat.

Slowly and carefully beat the hot syrup into the egg whites, pouring in a thin stream. Continue beating until the meringue has cooled, about 5 minutes.

In a separate bowl, beat the cream with the almond extract until it reaches the consistency of sour cream. Fold the cream and almonds into the meringue. Place in a freezer-proof container. Cover and freeze overnight or until firm.

‹ • ›

Variations

CHERRY NOUGAT ICE CREAM Cover ½ cup dried cherries with brandy and let sit for 1 hour or until soft. Add the drained cherries along with the nuts and cream. Proceed with the recipe as directed.

CHOCOLATE NOUGAT ICE CREAM Add ½ cup shaved bittersweet chocolate along with the almonds and cream. Proceed with the recipe as directed.

NOUGAT PARFAIT ICE CREAM Swirl ½ cup caramel sauce into the finished ice cream. Take care not to overswirl or the sauce will "melt" into the ice cream. Streaks of caramel should be visible. Serve immediately or freeze until firm.

NUTMEG ICE CREAM

NUTMEG perks up the flavor of so many dishes, rarely overasserting itself. In this ice cream, the delicious flavor of nutmeg comes into its own.

½ cup sugar

2 large egg yolks

1 tablespoon cornstarch

1½ cups milk

1 teaspoon ground nutmeg

1½ cups light cream

In a medium mixing bowl, beat the sugar into the eggs until thickened and pale yellow. Beat in the cornstarch and set aside.

Bring the milk to a simmer in a heavy medium saucepan. Slowly beat the hot milk into the eggs and sugar. Pour the entire mixture back into the pan and place over low heat. Stir constantly with a whisk or wooden spoon until the custard thickens slightly. Be careful not to let the mixture boil or the eggs will scramble. Remove from the heat and pour the hot custard through a strainer into a large, clean bowl. Allow the custard to cool slightly, then stir in the nutmeg and cream. Cover and refrigerate until cold or overnight.

Stir the chilled custard, then freeze in 1 or 2 batches in your ice cream machine according to the manufacturer's instructions. When finished, the ice cream will be soft but ready to eat. For firmer ice cream, transfer to a freezer-safe container and freeze at least 2 hours.

Variations

AUTUMN ICE CREAM When the ice cream is semifrozen, add ¼ cup each of the following: chopped pitted prunes, chopped pitted dried dates, and chopped dried figs. Allow the machine to mix in the additional ingredients. Proceed with the recipe as directed.

NUTTY NUTMEG ICE CREAM Add 1 cup chopped toasted walnuts (see page xvi) to the machine when the ice cream is semifrozen. Allow the machine to mix in the nuts. Proceed with the recipe as directed.

continued

SHOOFLY PIE ICE CREAM Add 2 tablespoons molasses along with the sugar. Proceed with the recipe as directed, adding ¼ cup raisins and 4 crumbled graham crackers to the machine when the ice cream is semifrozen. Allow the machine to mix in the crackers.

OATMEAL ICE CREAM

MAKES ABOUT 1 QUART

FINALLY, ice cream for breakfast.

¾ cup sugar

3 large egg yolks

2 cups milk

½ cup rolled oats
(not instant)

½ teaspoon salt

½ teaspoon ground
cinnamon

1½ cups heavy cream

In a medium mixing bowl, beat the sugar into the egg yolks until thickened and pale yellow. Set aside.

Bring the milk to a boil in a heavy medium saucepan over medium heat. Add the oats, salt, and cinnamon. Reduce the heat and return the milk to a simmer. Cook for 10 minutes, stirring constantly, until the oatmeal is thick and creamy. Slowly beat the hot oatmeal into the eggs and sugar. Allow the mixture to cool slightly. Stir in the cream. Cover and refrigerate until cold or overnight.

Stir the chilled custard, then freeze in 1 or 2 batches in your ice cream machine according to the manufacturer's instructions. When finished, the ice cream will be soft but ready to eat. For firmer ice cream, transfer to a freezer-safe container and freeze at least 2 hours.

◄　•　►

Variations

OATMEAL BANANA ICE CREAM Thinly slice 2 small bananas. Toss with 2 tablespoons sugar. Let the fruit macerate at least 2 hours. Stir the fruit into the custard before freezing. Proceed with the recipe as directed.

OATMEAL BERRY ICE CREAM Toss 1 cup fresh raspberries with 2 tablespoons sugar. Let the fruit macerate at least 2 hours. Stir the fruit into the custard before freezing. Proceed with the recipe as directed.

OATMEAL CRUNCH ICE CREAM Add 1 cup crunchy granola to the machine when the ice cream is semifrozen. Allow the machine to mix in the granola. Proceed with the recipe as directed.

continued

OATMEAL RAISIN ICE CREAM Add 1 cup raisins to the machine when the ice cream is semifrozen. Allow the machine to mix in the raisins. Proceed with the recipe as directed.

OATMEAL SPICE ICE CREAM Add ¼ teaspoon ground nutmeg, ¼ teaspoon ground cardamom, and ⅛ teaspoon ground mace along with the cinnamon. Proceed with the recipe as directed.

ORANGE ICE CREAM

FOR a premium-tasting ice cream, use a premium brand of frozen orange juice concentrate. If you like texture, use the orange juice concentrate with pulp.

⅓ cup sugar

4 large egg yolks

1½ teaspoons all-purpose
flour

¼ teaspoon salt

1⅓ cups half-and-half

⅔ cup orange juice
concentrate, defrosted

1 cup heavy cream

In a medium mixing bowl, beat the sugar into the egg yolks until thickened and pale yellow. Beat in the flour and salt. Set aside.

Bring the half-and-half to a simmer in a heavy medium saucepan. Slowly beat the hot half-and-half into the eggs and sugar. Pour the entire mixture back into the pan and place over low heat. Stir constantly with a whisk or wooden spoon until the custard thickens slightly. Be careful not to let the mixture boil or the eggs will scramble. Remove from the heat and pour the hot custard through a strainer into a large, clean bowl. Allow the custard to cool slightly, then stir in the orange juice concentrate and cream. Cover and refrigerate until cold or overnight.

Stir the chilled custard, then freeze in 1 or 2 batches in your ice cream machine according to the manufacturer's instructions. When finished, the ice cream will be soft but ready to eat. For firmer ice cream, transfer to a freezer-safe container and freeze at least 2 hours.

◄ • ►

Variations

ORANGE CANDY CRUNCH ICE CREAM Add ½ cup crushed hard orange candies to the machine when the ice cream is semifrozen. Allow the machine to mix in the candy. Proceed with the recipe as directed.

ORANGE CHIP ICE CREAM Add 1 cup miniature chocolate chips to the machine when the ice cream is semifrozen. Allow the machine to mix in the chips. Proceed with the recipe as directed.

continued

ORANGE COOKIE ICE CREAM Add 1 cup crumbled ginger snaps to the machine when the ice cream is semifrozen. Allow the machine to mix in the cookies. Proceed with the recipe as directed.

ORANGE CORDIAL ICE CREAM Add ¼ cup orange liqueur before freezing. Proceed with the recipe as directed.

ORANGE-VANILLA SWIRL ICE CREAM Swirl 1 cup marshmallow creme into the finished ice cream. Take care not to overswirl or the sauce will "melt" into the ice cream. Streaks of marshmallow should be visible. Serve immediately or freeze until firm.

PASSION FRUIT ICE CREAM

PASSION fruit concentrate is often found in the freezer section of supermarkets. It's also available in bottles at most Asian and Latin American markets. You can also try Central Market in Austin, Texas (800-360-2552).

¾ cup sugar

4 large egg yolks

1 teaspoon all-purpose
   flour

1½ cups half-and-half

¾ cup passion fruit
   concentrate

1 cup heavy cream

1 teaspoon vanilla extract

In a medium mixing bowl, beat the sugar into the egg yolks until thickened and pale yellow. Beat in the flour and set aside.

Bring the half-and-half to a simmer in a heavy medium saucepan. Slowly beat the hot half-and-half into the eggs and sugar. Pour the entire mixture back into the pan and place over low heat. Stir constantly with a whisk or wooden spoon until the custard thickens slightly. Be careful not to let the mixture boil or the eggs will scramble. Remove from the heat and pour the hot custard through a strainer into a large, clean bowl. Allow the custard to cool slightly, then stir in the passion fruit concentrate, cream, and vanilla. Cover and refrigerate until cold or overnight.

Stir the chilled custard, then freeze in 1 or 2 batches in your ice cream machine according to the manufacturer's instructions. When finished, the ice cream will be soft but ready to eat. For firmer ice cream, transfer to a freezer-safe container and freeze at least 2 hours.

‹ • ›

Variations

PASSION FRUIT RASPBERRY SWIRL ICE CREAM Stir 2 tablespoons water into ½ cup raspberry jam to loosen it up. Swirl the jam into the finished ice cream. Take care not to overswirl or the jam will "melt" into the ice cream. Streaks of jam should be visible. Serve immediately or freeze until firm.

continued

PASSION FRUIT STRAWBERRY CRUNCH ICE CREAM Add ½ cup crumbled vanilla wafers to the machine when the ice cream is semifrozen. Allow the machine to mix in the cookies. Stir 2 tablespoons water into ½ cup strawberry jam to loosen it up. Swirl the jam into the finished ice cream. Take care not to overswirl or the jam will "melt" into the ice cream. Streaks of jam should be visible. Serve immediately or freeze until firm.

PASSION NUT ICE CREAM Add ½ cup each chopped toasted almonds (see page xvi) and pecans to the machine when the ice cream is semifrozen. Allow the machine to mix in the nuts. Proceed with the recipe as directed.

PASSION PINEAPPLE ICE CREAM Add ½ cup drained canned crushed pineapple to the custard before freezing. Proceed with the recipe as directed.

PEACH ICE CREAM

NOTHING beats the flavor of fresh peach ice cream. Commercially frozen peaches and canned peaches just don't have the same fresh, summer taste. So buy extra when they're at their peak; then peel, slice, and freeze your own.

3 large, sweet peaches,
  peeled and pitted
  (about 1 1/4 pounds)
1/4 cup peach nectar
Juice of 1/2 lemon
1/4 teaspoon salt
2/3 cup sugar
2 large eggs
2 tablespoons all-purpose
  flour
1 cup milk
1 cup heavy cream

Slice the peaches into eighths and place in a blender with the peach nectar, lemon juice, and salt. Blend until the peaches are pureed. Set aside.

In a medium mixing bowl, beat the sugar into the eggs until they are thickened and pale yellow. Beat in the flour. Set aside.

Bring the milk to a simmer in a heavy medium saucepan. Slowly beat the hot milk into the eggs and sugar. Pour the entire mixture back into the pan and place over low heat. Stir constantly with a whisk or wooden spoon until the custard thickens slightly. Be careful not to let the mixture boil or the eggs will scramble. Remove from the heat and pour the hot custard through a strainer into a large, clean bowl. Allow the custard to cool slightly, then mix in the peach puree and cream. Cover and refrigerate until cold or overnight.

Stir the chilled custard, then freeze in 1 or 2 batches in your ice cream machine according to the manufacturer's instructions. When finished, the ice cream will be soft but ready to eat. For firmer ice cream, transfer to a freezer-safe container and freeze at least 2 hours.

◄ • ►

Variations

PEACH GINGER ICE CREAM Add 2 tablespoons finely chopped crystallized ginger to the machine when the ice cream is semifrozen. Allow the machine to mix in the ginger. Proceed with the recipe as directed.

continued

PEACH MACAROON ICE CREAM Add 1 cup crumbled coconut macaroons to the machine when the ice cream is semifrozen. Allow the machine to mix in the cookies. Proceed with the recipe as directed.

PEACH MELBA ICE CREAM Add 1 cup fresh raspberries to the blender along with the peaches. Increase the sugar to ¾ cup. Proceed with the recipe as directed.

PEACH THYME ICE CREAM Add 2 teaspoons chopped fresh thyme to the blender along with the peaches. Proceed with the recipe as directed.

PEACH ICE CREAM, PHILADELPHIA STYLE

No custard stands in the way of the peach flavor in this simple-to-make ice cream, so only the sweetest, fresh peaches will do.

1½ cups heavy cream

⅓ cup sugar

2 large, sweet peaches, peeled and pitted

¼ cup peach nectar

¼ teaspoon vanilla extract

Heat the cream in a heavy medium saucepan over medium heat until small bubbles appear around the edge. Do not let the cream boil. Remove from the heat and add the sugar, stirring until the sugar dissolves completely. Cool to room temperature.

Cut the peaches into eighths and place in a blender with the peach nectar. Blend until the peaches are pureed. Stir the peach puree and vanilla into the cooled cream. Refrigerate until cold or overnight.

Freeze in 1 or 2 batches in your ice cream machine according to the manufacturer's instructions. When finished, the ice cream will be soft but ready to eat. For firmer ice cream, transfer to a freezer-safe container and freeze at least 2 hours.

‹ • ›

Variations

PEACH ALMOND ICE CREAM Add ¼ teaspoon almond extract to the blender along with the peaches. Proceed with the recipe as directed, adding ¼ cup chopped toasted almonds (see page xvi) to the machine when the ice cream is semifrozen. Allow the machine to mix in the nuts.

PEACH BERRY ICE CREAM Add 1 cup crushed blueberries to the cream before freezing. Proceed with the recipe as directed.

PEACH COOKIE ICE CREAM Add ¾ cup crushed oatmeal cookies to the machine when the ice cream is semifrozen. Allow the machine to mix in the cookies. Proceed with the recipe as directed.

continued

PEACH MINT ICE CREAM Add 2 tablespoons chopped fresh mint to the blender along with the peaches. Proceed with the recipe as directed.

PEACHY PEACH ICE CREAM Add 1 cup diced fresh peaches (peeled and pitted) to the cream before freezing. Proceed with the recipe as directed.

PEACHY PEPPER ICE CREAM Add 2 teaspoons crushed dried green peppercorns to the blender along with the peaches. Proceed with the recipe as directed.

PEANUT BUTTER ICE CREAM

THIS recipe works best with creamy peanut butter. Reduced-fat or home-made peanut butter doesn't work as well. If you prefer your peanut butter ice cream chunky, simply add a handful of chopped nuts at the end.

¾ cup sugar

3 large eggs

1 cup milk

½ cup creamy peanut
  butter

1½ cups heavy cream

2 teaspoons vanilla extract

In a medium mixing bowl, beat the sugar into the eggs until thickened and pale yellow. Set aside.

Bring the milk to a simmer in a heavy medium saucepan. Slowly beat the hot milk into the eggs and sugar. Pour the entire mixture back into the pan and place over low heat. Stir constantly with a whisk or wooden spoon until the custard thickens slightly. Be careful not to let the mixture boil or the eggs will scramble. Remove from the heat and beat in the peanut butter. Pour the hot custard through a strainer into a large, clean bowl. Allow the peanut butter custard to cool slightly. Stir in the cream and vanilla. Cover and refrigerate until cold or overnight.

Stir the chilled custard, then freeze in 1 or 2 batches in your ice cream machine according to the manufacturer's instructions. When finished, the ice cream will be soft but ready to eat. For firmer ice cream, transfer to a freezer-safe container and freeze at least 2 hours.

◂ • ▸

Variations

CHOCOLATE PEANUT BUTTER ICE CREAM Add ½ cup miniature chocolate chips to the machine when the ice cream is semifrozen. Allow the machine to mix in the chips. Proceed with the recipe as directed.

DOUBLE PEANUT BUTTER ICE CREAM Add 1 cup crumbled peanut butter cup candies to the machine when the ice cream is semifrozen. Allow the machine to mix in the candy. Proceed with the recipe as directed.

continued

GORP ICE CREAM Add ¾ cup soft raisins to the machine when the ice cream is semi-frozen. Allow the machine to mix in the raisins. Proceed with the recipe as directed.

P B AND J ICE CREAM Stir 2 tablespoons water into ½ cup grape jam to loosen it up. Swirl the jam into the finished ice cream. Take care not to overswirl or the jam will "melt" into the ice cream. Streaks of jam should be visible. Serve immediately or freeze until firm.

PEANUT BUTTER BANANA FLUFF ICE CREAM Thinly slice 2 small bananas and toss with 2 tablespoons sugar. Allow the fruit to macerate for ½ hour. Proceed with recipe as directed, mixing the bananas into the custard before freezing. Swirl ¾ cup marshmallow creme into the finished ice cream. Take care not to overswirl or the marshmallow will "melt" into the ice cream. Streaks of marshmallow should be visible. Serve immediately or freeze until firm.

PEANUT BUTTER COOKIE CRUNCH ICE CREAM Add 1 cup crumbled oatmeal cookies to the machine when the ice cream is semifrozen. Allow the machine to mix in the cookies. Proceed with the recipe as directed.

SWEET AND SALTY PEANUT BUTTER ICE CREAM Add ¾ cup chopped salted peanuts to the machine when the ice cream is semifrozen. Allow the machine to mix in the nuts. Proceed with the recipe as directed.

PINEAPPLE ICE CREAM

FRESH pineapple should not be used to make pineapple ice cream: a naturally occurring enzyme can curdle the milk. Canning pineapple neutralizes this enzyme and so canned pineapple works just fine.

one 16-ounce can
unsweetened pineapple
chunks, drained

½ teaspoon salt

1 cup sugar

1 cup milk

3 large egg yolks

1 cup heavy cream

½ teaspoon vanilla extract

Place the pineapple chunks and salt in a food processor and process until smooth, about 1 minute. Set aside.

Combine the sugar and milk in a heavy medium saucepan. Place over low heat and stir until the sugar is dissolved and the milk comes to a boil. Beat the hot milk into the egg yolks in a bowl. Pour the entire mixture back into the pan and place over low heat. Stir constantly with a whisk or wooden spoon until the custard thickens slightly. Be careful not to let the mixture boil or the eggs will scramble. Remove from the heat and pour the hot custard through a strainer into a large, clean bowl. Allow the custard to cool slightly, then stir in the pineapple puree, cream, and vanilla. Cover and refrigerate until cold or overnight.

Stir the chilled custard, then freeze in 1 or 2 batches in your ice cream machine according to the manufacturer's instructions. When finished, the ice cream will be soft but ready to eat. For firmer ice cream, transfer to a freezer-safe container and freeze at least 2 hours.

◂ • ▸

Variations

HAWAIIAN ICE CREAM Add ¾ cup chopped macadamia nuts to the machine when the ice cream is semifrozen. Allow the machine to mix in the nuts. Proceed with the recipe as directed.

PINEAPPLE CHERRY DREAM ICE CREAM Add ½ cup chopped maraschino cherries to the machine when the ice cream is semifrozen. Allow the machine to mix in the cherries. Proceed with the recipe as directed.

continued

PINEAPPLE COCONUT ICE CREAM Substitute unsweetened coconut milk for the dairy milk. Proceed with the recipe as directed, adding ½ cup toasted, sweetened coconut (see page xvi) to the machine when the ice cream is semifrozen. Allow the machine to mix in the coconut.

PINEAPPLE ORANGE ICE CREAM Add 1 cup drained mandarin orange sections to the pineapple before pureeing. Proceed with the recipe as directed.

SOUTHWESTERN PINEAPPLE ICE CREAM Add ½ cup chopped dried banana chips and ½ teaspoon crushed red pepper flakes to the machine when the ice cream is semi-frozen. Allow the machine to mix in the additional ingredients. Proceed with the recipe as directed.

PINE NUT ICE CREAM

MAKES ABOUT 1 QUART

PINE nuts, sometimes called pignoli nuts, are available in most supermarkets, or Italian and Asian specialty stores. Because of the high fat content of pine nuts, store them in the freezer to keep them fresh.

1 cup pine nuts

¾ cup sugar

2 large eggs

1 cup milk

¼ teaspoon salt

1½ cups heavy cream

½ teaspoon vanilla extract

Preheat the oven to 400°F. Spread the pine nuts in a single layer on a baking sheet and place in the oven until lightly toasted, 5 to 10 minutes. Take care not to burn the nuts.

Combine the hot nuts and the sugar in a food processor and process for 2 minutes or until the mixture is smooth. Add the eggs and process until well blended, about 30 seconds.

Bring the milk to a boil in a heavy medium saucepan. With the food processor running, slowly pour the hot milk into the nut mixture through the feed tube. Process 30 seconds or until the nut custard is smooth. Pour the entire mixture back into the pan and place over low heat. Stir constantly with a whisk or wooden spoon until the custard thickens slightly. Be careful not to let the mixture boil or the eggs will scramble. Remove from the heat and pour the hot nut custard through a strainer into a large, clean bowl. Allow the custard to cool slightly, then stir in the salt, cream, and vanilla. Cover and refrigerate until cold or overnight.

Stir the chilled custard, then freeze in 1 or 2 batches in your ice cream machine according to the manufacturer's instructions. When finished, the ice cream will be soft but ready to eat. For firmer ice cream, transfer to a freezer-safe container and freeze at least 2 hours.

‹ • ›

Variations

BLACK PINE ICE CREAM Add ¼ cup chopped black licorice candy to the machine when the ice cream is semifrozen. Allow the machine to mix in the candy. Proceed with the recipe as directed.

continued

HONEY NUT ICE CREAM Substitute ½ cup honey for ½ cup sugar. Proceed with the recipe as directed.

PINEY SEED ICE CREAM Add ½ cup unsalted sunflower seeds to the machine when the ice cream is semifrozen. Allow the machine to mix in the seeds. Proceed with the recipe as directed.

TIRAMISÙ ICE CREAM Add 1 teaspoon instant espresso powder to the milk before heating. Proceed with the recipe as directed, adding 1 cup crumbled biscotti to the machine when the ice cream is semifrozen. Allow the machine to mix in the biscotti.

PISTACHIO ICE CREAM, PHILADELPHIA STYLE

USE unsalted pistachios for best results. If you shell your own, avoid the nuts that have been dyed red.

½ cup plus 2 tablespoons shelled pistachio nuts

2 tablespoons light corn syrup

1 cup half-and-half

½ cup sugar

½ teaspoon vanilla extract

¼ teaspoon almond extract

¼ teaspoon salt

1 cup heavy cream

Place ½ cup of pistachio nuts and the corn syrup in a food processor. Process for 2 minutes or until the nuts are completely smooth.

Bring the half-and-half to a simmer in a small heavy saucepan. Add the sugar and stir until it is completely dissolved. Remove from the heat. With the food processor running, slowly pour the hot half-and-half into the nut puree through the feed tube. Process until the mixture is completely smooth. Pour the nut mixture through a strainer into a large clean bowl. Allow to cool slightly. Stir in the vanilla and almond extracts, salt, and cream. Refrigerate until cold or overnight.

Stir the chilled cream, then freeze in 1 or 2 batches in your ice cream machine according to the manufacturer's instructions, adding the remaining 2 tablespoons of nuts when the ice cream is semifrozen. Allow the machine to mix in the nuts. When finished, the ice cream will be soft but ready to eat. For firmer ice cream, transfer to a freezer-safe container and freeze at least 2 hours.

Variations

ITALIAN PISTACHIO ICE CREAM Add ½ cup chopped candied fruit to the machine when the ice cream is semifrozen. Allow the machine to mix in the fruit. Proceed with the recipe as directed.

PISTACHIO ANISE ICE CREAM Add 1 teaspoon fennel seeds along with the whole pistachios. Proceed with the recipe as directed.

continued

PISTACHIO CHOCOLATE CHIP ICE CREAM Add ½ cup miniature chocolate chips to the machine when the ice cream is semifrozen. Allow the machine to mix in the chips. Proceed with the recipe as directed.

PISTACHIO CHOCOLATE SWIRL ICE CREAM Swirl ½ cup chocolate syrup or chocolate sauce into the finished ice cream. Take care not to overswirl or the chocolate will "melt" into the ice cream. Streaks of chocolate should be visible. Serve immediately or freeze until firm.

PISTACHIO MACAROON ICE CREAM Add ¾ cup crumbled coconut macaroons to the machine when the ice cream is semifrozen. Allow the machine to mix in the macaroons. Proceed with the recipe as directed.

PRUNE ICE CREAM

MAKES ABOUT 1 QUART

T HE flavors of the prunes and Cognac blend nicely in ice cream. For a more pronounced prune flavor, try Armagnac instead. If you don't care for alcohol, simply use prune juice.

12 small pitted prunes, cut
   into quarters

1 cup sugar

3 large eggs

1 tablespoon all-purpose
   flour

1½ cups half-and-half

1 cup heavy cream

¼ cup Cognac or prune
   juice

Cover the prunes with boiling water and set aside to soften for 1 hour.

In a medium mixing bowl, beat the sugar into the eggs until thickened and pale yellow. Beat in the flour and set aside.

Bring the half-and-half to a boil in a heavy medium saucepan. Slowly beat the hot half-and-half into the eggs and sugar. Pour the entire mixture back into the pan and place over low heat. Stir constantly with a whisk or wooden spoon until the custard thickens slightly. Be careful not to let the mixture boil or the eggs will scramble. Remove from the heat and pour the hot custard through a strainer into a large, clean bowl. Allow the custard to cool slightly. Drain the prunes, chop fine, and add them to the custard. Stir in the cream and Cognac or prune juice. Cover and refrigerate until cold or overnight.

Stir the chilled custard, then freeze in 1 or 2 batches in your ice cream machine according to the manufacturer's instructions. When finished, the ice cream will be soft but ready to eat. For firmer ice cream, transfer to a freezer-safe container and freeze at least 2 hours.

‹ • ›

Variations

PRUNE AND CHEESE DANISH ICE CREAM Add ½ cup crumbled coffee cake to the machine when the ice cream is semifrozen. Allow the machine to mix in the cake. Mix ¾ cup ricotta with 3 tablespoons sugar and 1 tablespoon amaretto liqueur or almond syrup. Swirl this mixture into the finished ice cream. Take care not to overswirl or the cheese will "melt" into the ice cream. Streaks of cheese should be visible. Serve immediately or freeze until firm.

PRUNE APRICOT ICE CREAM Substitute dried apricot halves for half the prunes. Proceed with the recipe as directed.

WINTER FRUITS ICE CREAM Add 2 tablespoons chopped dried cherries, 2 tablespoons raisins, 2 tablespoons chopped dried apples, and 2 chopped dried figs to the machine when the ice cream is semifrozen. Allow the machine to mix in the fruit. Proceed with the recipe as directed.

PUMPKIN ICE CREAM

R EAD the label carefully when you're buying canned pumpkin. Look for solid-pack pumpkin, not pumpkin pie mix.

½ cup light brown sugar

½ cup light corn syrup

5 large egg yolks

1 tablespoon cornstarch

½ teaspoon ground
  cinnamon

¼ teaspoon ground
  nutmeg

¼ teaspoon ground ginger

1 cup half-and-half

One 15-ounce can solid-
  pack pumpkin

1 cup heavy cream

1 teaspoon vanilla extract

In a medium mixing bowl, beat the brown sugar and corn syrup into the egg yolks until thickened and pale yellow. Beat in the cornstarch, cinnamon, nutmeg, and ginger. Set aside.

Bring the half-and-half to a simmer in a large, heavy saucepan. Slowly beat the hot half-and-half into the eggs and sugar. Pour the entire mixture back into the pan and place over low heat. Stir constantly with a whisk or wooden spoon until the custard thickens slightly. Be careful not to let the mixture boil or the eggs will scramble. Remove from the heat and beat in the canned pumpkin. Pour the hot custard through a strainer into a large, clean bowl. Allow the custard to cool slightly, then stir in the cream and vanilla. Cover and refrigerate until cold or overnight.

Stir the chilled custard, then freeze in 1 or 2 batches in your ice cream machine according to the manufacturer's instructions. When finished, the ice cream will be soft but ready to eat. For firmer ice cream, transfer to a freezer-safe container and freeze at least 2 hours.

◄ • ►

Variations

PUMPKIN PIE ICE CREAM Add 1 teaspoon grated fresh orange zest along with the vanilla. Proceed with the recipe as directed. Add ½ cup crumbled ginger snaps to the machine when the ice cream is semifrozen. Allow the machine to mix in the cookies.

continued

PUMPKIN RAISIN ICE CREAM Add 1 cup soft raisins to the machine when the ice cream is semifrozen. Allow the machine to mix in the raisins. Proceed with the recipe as directed.

PUMPKIN RUM ICE CREAM Add ⅓ cup dark rum to the custard before freezing. Proceed with the recipe as directed.

PUMPKIN SEED ICE CREAM Add 1 cup unsalted shelled pumpkin seeds to the machine when the ice cream is semifrozen. Allow the machine to mix in the seeds. Proceed with the recipe as directed.

PURPLE PLUM ICE CREAM

CANNED purple plums in heavy syrup almost always have pits. Don't forget to remove them all or you might ruin the blade of your food processor.

One 15-ounce can purple
plums, drained and
pitted, with syrup
reserved

½ teaspoon salt

2 teaspoons fresh lemon
juice

½ cup sugar

3 large egg yolks

1 cup milk

1 cup heavy cream

Place the plums in a food processor. Add the salt, lemon juice, and ½ cup of the reserved plum syrup. Process until the fruit is pureed. In a medium mixing bowl, beat the sugar into the egg yolks until thickened and pale yellow. Set aside.

Bring the milk to a simmer in a heavy medium saucepan. Slowly beat the hot milk into the eggs and sugar. Pour the entire mixture back into the pan and place over low heat. Stir constantly with a whisk or wooden spoon until the custard thickens slightly. Be careful not to let the mixture boil or the eggs will scramble. Remove from the heat, then pour the hot custard through a strainer into a large, clean bowl. Allow the custard to cool slightly, then stir in the plum puree and cream. Cover and refrigerate until cold or overnight.

Stir the chilled custard, then freeze in 1 or 2 batches in your ice cream machine according to the manufacturer's instructions. When finished, the ice cream will be soft but ready to eat. For firmer ice cream, transfer to a freezer-safe container and freeze at least 2 hours.

‹ • ›

Variations

PLUM ALMOND ICE CREAM Add ¼ teaspoon almond extract to the food processor with the plums. Proceed with the recipe as directed, adding ½ cup slivered almonds to the machine when the ice cream is semifrozen. Allow the machine to mix in the nuts.

continued

PLUM COOKIE ICE CREAM Add 1 cup crumbled Chinese almond cookies to the machine when the ice cream is semifrozen. Allow the machine to mix in the cookies. Proceed with the recipe as directed.

PLUM LEMONGRASS ICE CREAM Smash a 6-inch stalk of lemongrass with the back of a heavy knife and add to the milk before heating. Bring to a simmer. Remove from the heat and let steep for 20 minutes. Discard the lemongrass and proceed with the recipe as directed.

PLUM TARRAGON ICE CREAM Add 2 tablespoons chopped fresh tarragon to the food processor along with the plums. Proceed with the recipe as directed.

PLUM WINE ICE CREAM Add ½ cup plum wine before freezing. Proceed with the recipe as directed.

RASPBERRY ICE CREAM

Frozen raspberries work just as well as fresh berries in this recipe. For best results, measure berries by weight instead of by volume.

3 large egg yolks

1 cup sugar

½ cup water

¾ pound red raspberries
(3 to 4 cups fresh berries)

¼ teaspoon salt

1 tablespoon fresh lemon
juice

2 cups half-and-half

Place the egg yolks in a food processor and set aside. Combine the sugar and water in a small, heavy saucepan and place over low heat. Stir until the sugar dissolves. Turn the heat to high and bring the syrup to a boil. Boil without stirring for 3 minutes. With the food processor running, slowly pour the hot syrup into the egg yolks through the feed tube. (The eggs are cooked by the hot sugar syrup.) Process until the mixture is thickened and pale yellow. Turn off the processor and add the raspberries, salt, and lemon juice. Process until the fruit is pureed and the mixture is smooth.

If desired, pour the entire contents through a strainer or food mill to remove the seeds. Stir in the half-and-half. Cover and refrigerate until cold or overnight.

Stir the chilled custard, then freeze in 1 or 2 batches in your ice cream machine according to the manufacturer's instructions. When finished, the ice cream will be soft but ready to eat. This ice cream will retain a soft consistency even after left in the freezer overnight.

◂ • ▸

Variations

DOUBLE RASPBERRY SWIRL ICE CREAM Stir 2 tablespoons water into ¾ cup raspberry jam to loosen it up. Swirl the jam into the finished ice cream. Take care not to over-swirl or the jam will "melt" into the ice cream. Streaks of jam should be visible. Serve immediately or freeze until firm.

continued

RASPBERRY–BUTTER CRUNCH ICE CREAM Add 1 cup crushed peanut brittle to the machine when the ice cream is semifrozen. Allow the machine to mix in the candy. Proceed with the recipe as directed.

RASPBERRY CHEESECAKE ICE CREAM Add ½ cup no-bake cheesecake mix to the food processor along with the berries. Proceed with the recipe as directed, adding 6 crumbled graham crackers to the machine when the ice cream is semifrozen. Allow the machine to mix in the crackers.

RASPBERRY CORDIAL ICE CREAM Add ½ cup raspberry liqueur before freezing. Proceed with the recipe as directed.

RASPBERRY HAZELNUT ICE CREAM Add ¼ cup hazelnut liqueur or syrup before freezing. Proceed with the recipe as directed, adding ¾ cup chopped toasted hazelnuts (see page xvi) to the machine when the ice cream is semifrozen. Allow the machine to mix in the nuts.

RASPBERRY TRUFFLE ICE CREAM Add ½ pound chopped chocolate to the machine when the ice cream is semifrozen. Allow the machine to mix in the candy. Proceed with the recipe as directed.

RED BEAN ICE CREAM

MAKES ABOUT 1 QUART

SWEETENED red bean paste is available in many Asian markets. The texture is somewhat grainy, but pleasant.

½ cup sugar

3 large egg yolks

1 cup milk

1½ cups Chinese
  sweetened red bean
  paste

1½ cups heavy cream

In a medium mixing bowl, beat the sugar into the egg yolks until thickened and pale yellow. Set aside.

Bring the milk to a boil in a heavy medium saucepan. Slowly beat the hot milk into the eggs and sugar. Pour the entire mixture back into the pan and place over low heat. Stir constantly with a whisk or wooden spoon until the custard thickens slightly. Be careful not to let the mixture boil or the eggs will scramble. Remove from the heat and beat in the red bean paste. Pour the hot bean custard through a strainer into a large, clean bowl. Allow the custard to cool slightly, then stir in the cream. Cover and refrigerate until cold or overnight.

Stir the chilled custard, then freeze in 1 or 2 batches in your ice cream machine according to the manufacturer's instructions. When finished, the ice cream will be soft but ready to eat. For firmer ice cream, transfer to a freezer-safe container and freeze at least 2 hours.

Variations

RED BEAN ALMOND CRUNCH ICE CREAM Add ¼ teaspoon almond extract along with the red bean paste. Proceed with the recipe as directed, adding 1 cup crumbled Chinese almond cookies to the machine when the ice cream is semifrozen. Allow the machine to mix in the cookies.

SHANGHAI ICE CREAM Add 2 tablespoons finely chopped crystallized ginger and ½ cup crumbled ginger snaps to the machine when the ice cream is semifrozen. Allow the machine to mix in the additional ingredients. Proceed with the recipe as directed.

continued

SPICED RED BEAN ICE CREAM Add ½ teaspoon ground cinnamon and ¼ teaspoon ground nutmeg along with the red bean paste. Proceed with the recipe as directed.

THAI RED BEAN ICE CREAM Add 2 teaspoons hot chile paste and 2 tablespoons minced fresh basil along with the red bean paste. Proceed with the recipe as directed.

RHUBARB ICE CREAM

WHETHER you use fresh or frozen rhubarb, you'll have to cook it first. It's a little bit of work, but worth every mouthful.

1 pound rhubarb, cut into
 ½-inch pieces

1 cup water

Juice of 1 lime

½ cup light corn syrup

⅔ cup sugar

1 large egg plus 1
 additional egg yolk

2 teaspoons cornstarch

1 cup milk

1 cup heavy cream

Combine the rhubarb, water, and lime juice in a medium saucepan and place over low heat. Bring to a simmer and cook, stirring occasionally, until the rhubarb has broken down and resembles thick applesauce, about 10 minutes.

Add the corn syrup, return to a simmer, and cook 2 minutes longer. Push the rhubarb through a sieve with the back of a wooden spoon, or pass it through a food mill, yielding about 1¼ cups of puree. Set aside.

In a medium mixing bowl, beat the sugar into the egg and egg yolk until thickened and pale yellow. Beat in the cornstarch. Set aside.

Bring the milk to a simmer in a heavy medium saucepan. Slowly beat the hot milk into the eggs and sugar. Pour the entire mixture back into the pan and place over low heat. Stir constantly with a whisk or wooden spoon until the custard thickens slightly. Be careful not to let the mixture boil or the eggs will scramble. Remove from the heat and pour the hot custard through a strainer into a large, clean bowl. Allow the custard to cool slightly, then stir in the rhubarb puree and cream. Cover and refrigerate until cold or overnight.

Stir the chilled custard, then freeze in 1 or 2 batches in your ice cream machine according to the manufacturer's instructions. When finished, the ice cream will be soft but ready to eat. For firmer ice cream, transfer to a freezer-safe container and freeze at least 2 hours.

continued

Variations

KENTUCKY RHUBARB PIE ICE CREAM Substitute bourbon for the water and proceed with the recipe as directed, adding ¾ cup crumbled graham crackers or baked pie crust to the machine when the ice cream is semifrozen. Allow the machine to mix in the crackers.

PEACHY RHUBARB ICE CREAM Reduce the rhubarb to ¾ pound. Add 1 large peach (peeled, pitted, and thinly sliced) to the pan along with the rhubarb. Proceed with the recipe as directed.

RASPBERRY RHUBARB ICE CREAM Reduce the rhubarb to ¾ pound. Add 1 cup raspberries to the pan along with the rhubarb. Proceed with the recipe as directed.

STRAWBERRY RHUBARB ICE CREAM Add 1½ cups thinly sliced strawberries to the pan along with the rhubarb. Increase the sugar by 2 tablespoons and proceed with the recipe as directed.

RICE ICE CREAM

MAKES ABOUT 1 QUART

THE secret of this Florentine ice cream is the rice—Arborio, the short-grain Italian rice that cooks up richer and creamier than long-grain American rice. Long-grain rice will work if that's what you have, but stay away from instant rice.

¾ cup cooked Arborio rice (follow directions on the package)
2 cups milk
¾ cup sugar
2 large eggs
1½ cups heavy cream
¼ teaspoon vanilla extract
¼ teaspoon ground anise or fennel seed

Combine the cooked rice, milk, and sugar in a heavy medium saucepan and place over medium heat. Stir until the sugar is dissolved and the milk comes to a simmer.

Lower the heat and simmer, stirring occasionally until the mixture is thick and creamy, about 30 minutes. The rice should have a porridgelike consistency. Stir constantly during the last few minutes to prevent sticking and burning. Slowly beat the hot rice into the eggs in a large mixing bowl. Allow the mixture to cool slightly. Stir in the cream, vanilla, and anise. Cover and refrigerate until cold or overnight.

Stir the chilled custard, then freeze in 1 or 2 batches in your ice cream machine according to the manufacturer's instructions. When finished, the ice cream will be soft but ready to eat. For firmer ice cream, transfer to a freezer-safe container and freeze at least 2 hours.

‹ • • ›

Variations

COFFEE RICE ICE CREAM Mix 1 tablespoon instant espresso powder into the milk along with the rice and sugar. Proceed with the recipe as directed.

GOLDEN RAISIN RICE ICE CREAM Add ½ cup golden raisins to the pan along with the rice. Proceed with the recipe as directed.

continued

HAZELNUT RICE ICE CREAM Add ¼ cup hazelnut syrup or liqueur before freezing. Proceed with the recipe as directed, adding ½ cup chopped toasted hazelnuts (see page xvi) to the machine when the ice cream is semifrozen. Allow the machine to mix in the nuts.

LEMON RICE ICE CREAM Add 2 teaspoons grated fresh lemon zest and ½ teaspoon lemon extract to the hot rice before adding the eggs. Proceed with the recipe as directed.

RUM RICE ICE CREAM Add ⅓ cup dark rum before freezing. Proceed with the recipe as directed.

RUM RAISIN ICE CREAM

MAKES ABOUT 1 QUART

IF you are going to the trouble to make your own rum raisin ice cream, use only plump, soft raisins and premium, golden rum.

1 cup plump, soft raisins

¼ cup gold rum

1 cup sugar

3 large eggs

1 tablespoon all-purpose flour

1½ cups half-and-half

1 cup heavy cream

Cover the raisins with the rum and let sit for 1 hour.

In a medium mixing bowl, beat the sugar into the eggs until thickened and pale yellow. Beat in the flour and set aside.

Bring the half-and-half to a boil in a heavy medium saucepan. Slowly beat the hot half-and-half into the eggs and sugar. Pour the entire mixture back into the pan and place over low heat. Stir constantly with a whisk or wooden spoon until the custard thickens slightly. Be careful not to let the mixture boil or the eggs will scramble. Remove from the heat and pour the hot custard through a strainer into a large, clean bowl. Allow the custard to cool slightly, then stir in the raisins, rum, and cream. Cover and refrigerate until cold or overnight.

Stir the chilled custard, then freeze in 1 or 2 batches in your ice cream machine according to the manufacturer's instructions. When finished, the ice cream will be soft but ready to eat. For firmer ice cream, transfer to a freezer-safe container and freeze at least 2 hours.

Variations

CHOCOLATE RUM RAISIN ICE CREAM Substitute chocolate-covered raisins for regular raisins. Do not soak the raisins in the rum. Proceed with the recipe as directed.

ITALIAN RAISIN ICE CREAM Substitute grappa for the rum and proceed with the recipe as directed.

RUM RAISIN CRUNCH ICE CREAM Add ¾ cup crumbled biscotti to the machine when the ice cream is semifrozen. Allow the machine to mix in the biscotti. Proceed with the recipe as directed.

SAFFRON ICE CREAM

MAKES ABOUT 1 QUART

SAFFRON is expensive, but a little goes a long way. Just ¼ teaspoon of crumbled saffron threads is enough to make this ice cream bright yellow and flavorful. Use as little as ⅛ teaspoon if you prefer a milder saffron taste and a lower grocery bill.

⅛ to ¼ teaspoon crumbled
saffron threads

1½ cups milk

1¼ cups sugar

6 large egg yolks

2 teaspoons all-purpose
flour

¼ teaspoon salt

1½ cups heavy cream

Combine the saffron and milk in a heavy medium saucepan and bring to a simmer over low heat. Remove from the heat, cover, and allow the saffron to steep in the milk for 30 minutes.

Beat the sugar into the egg yolks until thickened and pale yellow. Beat in the flour and salt. Set aside.

Return the milk to a simmer, then slowly beat the hot milk into the eggs and sugar. Pour the entire mixture back into the pan and place over low heat. Stir constantly with a whisk or wooden spoon until the custard thickens slightly. Be careful not to let the mixture boil or the eggs will scramble. Remove from the heat and pour the hot saffron custard through a strainer into a large, clean bowl. Allow the custard to cool slightly, then stir in the cream. Cover and refrigerate until cold or overnight.

Stir the chilled custard, then freeze in 1 or 2 batches in your ice cream machine according to the manufacturer's instructions. When finished, the ice cream will be soft but ready to eat. For firmer ice cream, transfer to a freezer-safe container and freeze at least 2 hours.

Variations

SAFFRON CURRANT CRUNCH ICE CREAM Add ¼ cup dried currants and ¼ cup chopped almonds to the machine when the ice cream is semifrozen. Proceed with the recipe as directed.

SAFFRON GINGER DATE ICE CREAM Add 2 tablespoons chopped fresh ginger to the milk along with saffron. Proceed with the recipe as directed, adding ¼ cup chopped dried dates to the machine when the ice cream is semifrozen.

STRAWBERRY ICE CREAM

■F you can't find fresh berries, use premium, whole, frozen berries without syrup, defrosted.

3 heaping cups
  strawberries

¼ teaspoon salt

⅓ cup sugar

2 large eggs

1½ cups half-and-half

½ cup heavy cream

1 teaspoon vanilla extract

Puree the strawberries with the salt in a food processor or food mill. There should be about 2 cups of puree. Set aside.

In a medium mixing bowl, beat the sugar into the eggs until thickened and pale yellow. Set aside.

Bring the half-and-half to a simmer in a heavy medium saucepan. Slowly beat the hot half-and-half into the eggs and sugar. Pour the entire mixture back into the pan and place over low heat. Stir constantly with a whisk or wooden spoon until the custard thickens slightly. Be careful not to let the mixture boil or the eggs will scramble. Remove from the heat and pour the hot custard through a strainer into a large, clean bowl. Allow the custard to cool slightly, then stir in the strawberry puree, cream, and vanilla. Cover and refrigerate until cold or overnight.

Stir the chilled custard, then freeze in 1 or 2 batches in your ice cream machine according to the manufacturer's instructions. When finished, the ice cream will be soft but ready to eat. For firmer ice cream, transfer to a freezer-safe container and freeze at least 2 hours.

◂ • ▸

Variations

STRAWBERRY ALMOND ICE CREAM Add ½ teaspoon almond extract along with the vanilla. Proceed with the recipe as directed, adding 1 cup slivered almonds to the machine when the ice cream is semifrozen.

STRAWBERRY BLACK PEPPER ICE CREAM Add 2 teaspoons coarsely ground black pepper to the custard before freezing. Proceed with the recipe as directed.

STRAWBERRY CABERNET ICE CREAM Bring 2 cups red wine (cabernet sauvignon) to a boil in a small, heavy saucepan. Boil until the wine is reduced to ½ cup, thick and syrupy. Add this reduced wine to the strawberry puree and proceed with the recipe as directed.

STRAWBERRY VINEGAR ICE CREAM Add 3 tablespoons aged balsamic vinegar to the strawberry puree. Proceed with the recipe as directed. Optional: add 2 teaspoons coarsely ground black pepper to the custard before freezing.

STRAWBERRY ICE CREAM, PHILADELPHIA STYLE

THIS version of strawberry ice cream doesn't rely on a custard for texture or taste, so use only sweet and juicy fresh strawberries.

2 cups heavy cream

⅓ cup sugar

3 cups fresh strawberries

¼ cup milk

Heat the cream in a large heavy saucepan over medium heat until small bubbles appear around the edge. Do not let the cream boil. Remove from the heat and add the sugar, stirring until the sugar dissolves completely. Cool to room temperature.

Meanwhile, cut the berries into quarters and place in a blender with the milk. Blend until the berries are pureed. Add the puree to the cooled cream. Refrigerate until cold or overnight. Freeze in 1 or 2 batches in your ice cream machine according to the manufacturer's instructions. When finished, the ice cream will be soft but ready to eat. For firmer ice cream, transfer to a freezer-safe container and freeze at least 2 hours.

◄ • ►

Variations

STRAWBERRY BANANA ICE CREAM Thinly slice 2 small bananas and toss with 2 tablespoons sugar and 1 tablespoon banana liqueur or water. Allow the fruit to macerate for 1 hour. Combine the banana mixture with the cream before freezing. Proceed with the recipe as directed.

STRAWBERRY GUM DROP ICE CREAM Add ¼ cup gummy-strawberries to the machine when the ice cream is semifrozen. Allow the machine to mix in the candy. Proceed with the recipe as directed.

STRAWBERRY MINT ICE CREAM Add 2 teaspoons minced fresh mint leaves before freezing. Proceed with the recipe as directed.

STRAWBERRY WAFER ICE CREAM Add 1 cup crushed sugar wafers to the machine when the ice cream is semifrozen. Allow the machine to mix in the wafers. Proceed with the recipe as directed.

SWEET POTATO ICE CREAM

ROASTED sweet potatoes have a rich caramel flavor that you can't get from boiled or canned sweet potatoes.

2 medium sweet potatoes

½ cup sugar

2 large eggs

¼ cup light corn syrup

½ teaspoon salt

1 cup half-and-half

1 cup heavy cream

½ teaspoon vanilla extract

Scrub the sweet potatoes and bake them in a 400°F oven for 1 hour, or until soft. When cool enough to handle, peel and mash the potatoes. You should have about 1¼ cups of mashed sweet potato. Set aside.

In a medium mixing bowl, beat the sugar into the eggs until thickened and pale yellow. Beat in the corn syrup and salt. Set aside.

Bring the half-and-half to a simmer in a large, heavy saucepan. Slowly beat the hot half-and-half into the eggs and sugar. Pour the entire mixture back into the pan and place over low heat. Stir constantly with a whisk or wooden spoon until the custard thickens slightly. Be careful not to let the mixture boil or the eggs will scramble. Remove from the heat and beat in the potato puree. Pour the hot potato custard through a strainer into a large, clean bowl. Allow the custard to cool slightly, then stir in the cream and vanilla. Cover and refrigerate until cold or overnight.

Stir the chilled custard, then freeze in 1 or 2 batches in your ice cream machine according to the manufacturer's instructions. When finished, the ice cream will be soft but ready to eat. For firmer ice cream, transfer to a freezer-safe container and freeze at least 2 hours.

‹ • ›

Variations

SOUTHERN SWEET POTATO SOUFFLÉ ICE CREAM Add ½ teaspoon ground cinnamon and ¼ teaspoon ground nutmeg along with the salt. Proceed with the recipe as directed, adding ½ cup mini-marshmallows and ½ cup drained crushed canned pineapple to the machine when the ice cream is semifrozen. Allow the machine to mix in the additional ingredients.

continued

SWEET POTATO PIE ICE CREAM Substitute maple syrup for the corn syrup. Add ½ teaspoon ground cinnamon, ¼ teaspoon ground nutmeg, ⅛ teaspoon ground mace along with the salt. Proceed with the recipe as directed, adding 6 crumbled graham crackers to the machine when the ice cream is semifrozen. Allow the machine to mix in the crackers.

SWEET POTATO RAISIN ICE CREAM Add ¾ cup golden raisins to the machine when the ice cream is semifrozen. Allow the machine to mix in the raisins. Proceed with the recipe as directed.

SWEET SOUTHERN COMFORT ICE CREAM Add ⅓ cup Southern Comfort before freezing. Proceed with the recipe as directed.

VANILLA ICE CREAM #1 (PURE AND SIMPLE)

THIS ice cream is best served right out of the machine while it's still soft and creamy. It's so rich, it doesn't even need a topping.

⅔ cup sugar

2 large eggs

2 tablespoons all-purpose
  flour

¼ teaspoon salt

1⅔ cups milk

1 cup heavy cream

2 teaspoons vanilla extract

In a medium mixing bowl, beat the sugar into the eggs until thickened and pale yellow. Beat in the flour and salt. Set aside.

Bring the milk to a simmer in a heavy medium saucepan. Slowly beat the hot milk into the eggs and sugar. Pour the entire mixture back into the pan and place over low heat. Stir constantly with a whisk or wooden spoon until the custard thickens slightly. Be careful not to let the mixture boil or the eggs will scramble. Remove from the heat and pour the hot custard through a strainer into a large, clean bowl. Allow the custard to cool slightly, then stir in the cream and vanilla. Cover and refrigerate until cold or overnight.

Stir the chilled custard, then freeze in 1 or 2 batches in your ice cream machine according to the manufacturer's instructions. When finished, the ice cream will be soft but ready to eat. For firmer ice cream, transfer to a freezer-safe container and freeze at least 2 hours.

◂ • •

Variations

BUTTERSCOTCH CREAM PIE ICE CREAM Add ¾ cup mini-marshmallows, ¼ cup butterscotch chips, and 6 crumbled graham crackers to the machine when the ice cream is semifrozen. Allow the machine to mix in the additional ingredients. Proceed with the recipe as directed.

CHERRY VANILLA ICE CREAM Add ½ cup maraschino cherries to the machine when the ice cream is semifrozen. Allow the machine to mix in the fruit. Proceed with the recipe as directed.

continued

VANILLA CHOCOLATE NUT ICE CREAM Add ¾ cup chocolate-covered peanuts or almonds to the machine when the ice cream is semifrozen. Allow the machine to mix in the candy. Proceed with the recipe as directed.

VANILLA ICE CREAM #2 (EXTRA RICH AND CREAMY)

WITH so many egg yolks in this recipe, it's easy to "scramble" this custard. So either use a very low heat or cook this custard in a double boiler or stainless steel bowl set over a pot of simmering water. This takes a bit longer, but it is a safe way to ensure a smooth custard.

1 cup sugar

¼ teaspoon salt

7 large egg yolks

1½ cups half-and-half

1 cup heavy cream

1 tablespoon vanilla extract

In a medium mixing bowl, beat the sugar and salt into the egg yolks until thickened and pale yellow. Set aside.

Bring the half-and-half to a simmer in a heavy medium sauce pan. Slowly beat the hot half-and-half into the eggs and sugar. Pour the entire mixture back into the pan and place over very low heat or in a double boiler. Stir constantly with a whisk or wooden spoon until the custard thickens slightly. Be careful not to let the mixture boil or the eggs will scramble. Remove from the heat and pour the hot custard through a strainer into a large, clean bowl. Allow the custard to cool slightly, then stir in the cream and vanilla. Cover and refrigerate until cold or overnight.

Stir the chilled custard, then freeze in 1 or 2 batches in your ice cream machine according to the manufacturer's instructions. When finished, the ice cream will be soft but ready to eat. For firmer ice cream, transfer to a freezer-safe container and freeze at least 2 hours.

‹ • ›

Variations

BITTERSWEET CHOCOLATE–LACED VANILLA ICE CREAM
Add 1 cup shaved bittersweet chocolate to the machine when the ice cream is semifrozen. Allow the machine to mix in the chocolate. Proceed with the recipe as directed.

continued

VANILLA BEAN ICE CREAM Slit 1 vanilla bean lengthwise. Scrape out the seeds and place both bean and seeds in saucepan with the half-and-half. Bring to a simmer over medium heat. Remove from the heat, cover, and steep for 10 minutes. Remove the vanilla bean and proceed with the recipe as directed, omitting the vanilla extract.

VANILLA MOCHA BEAN ICE CREAM Add ¾ cup chocolate-covered espresso beans to the machine when the ice cream is semifrozen. Allow the machine to mix in the beans. Proceed with the recipe as directed.

WHITE RUSSIAN ICE CREAM Add ¼ cup vodka and ¼ cup coffee liqueur before freezing. Proceed with the recipe as directed.

VANILLA ICE CREAM #3 (LOWER FAT)

SWEETENED condensed milk replaces cream and sugar in this recipe, reducing fat and calories. Low-fat or fat-free sweetened condensed milk will reduce the fat and calorie contents even further.

2 cups milk (2% or skim)

2 large eggs plus 2 egg
    yolks, lightly beaten

One 14-ounce can
    sweetened condensed
    milk

4 teaspoons vanilla extract

Bring the milk to a simmer in a heavy medium saucepan. Slowly beat the hot milk into the eggs in a medium mixing bowl. Pour the entire mixture back into the pan and place over low heat. Stir constantly with a whisk or wooden spoon until the custard thickens slightly. Be careful not to let the mixture boil or the eggs will scramble. Remove from the heat and pour the hot custard through a strainer into a large, clean bowl. Allow the custard to cool slightly, then stir in the sweetened condensed milk and vanilla. Cover and refrigerate until cold or overnight.

Stir the chilled custard, then freeze in 1 or 2 batches in your ice cream machine according to the manufacturer's instructions. When finished, the ice cream will be soft but ready to eat. For firmer ice cream, transfer to a freezer-safe container and freeze at least 2 hours.

‹ • ›

Variations

VANILLA CRUNCH ICE CREAM Add 1 cup frosted corn flake cereal to the machine when the ice cream is semifrozen. Allow the machine to mix in the cereal. Proceed with the recipe as directed.

VANILLA MARMALADE SWIRL ICE CREAM Stir 2 tablespoons orange liqueur into ¾ cup orange marmalade to loosen it up. Swirl the marmalade into the finished ice cream. Take care not to overswirl or the marmalade will "melt" into the ice cream. Streaks of orange should be visible. Serve immediately or freeze until firm.

continued

VANILLA ROSE ICE CREAM Add 1 tablespoon rose water along with the vanilla extract. Proceed with the recipe as directed, adding 2 tablespoons crushed candied rose petals to the machine when the ice cream is semifrozen. Allow the machine to mix in the flowers.

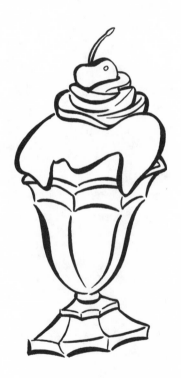

VANILLA ICE CREAM, PHILADELPHIA STYLE

MAKES ABOUT 1 QUART

THIS is one of the oldest ways to make ice cream and still one of the easiest. All it takes is three ingredients. Heating the cream before adding the sugar makes a smoother, richer ice cream.

3 cups heavy cream

¾ cup plus 2 tablespoons
sugar

2 teaspoons vanilla extract

Heat the cream in a large heavy saucepan over medium heat until small bubbles appear around the edge. Do not let the cream boil. Remove from the heat and add the sugar, stirring until the sugar is completely dissolved. Allow the cream to cool slightly, then stir in the vanilla. Cover and refrigerate until cold or overnight.

Freeze in 1 or 2 batches in your ice cream machine according to the manufacturer's instructions. When finished, the ice cream will be soft but ready to eat. For firmer ice cream, transfer to a freezer-safe container and freeze at least 2 hours.

◂ • ▸

Variations

VANILLA CANDY BAR ICE CREAM Add 2 chopped candy bars of your choice to the machine when the ice cream is semifrozen. Allow the machine to mix in the candy. Proceed with the recipe as directed. Candy bar suggestions include Snickers, Milky Way, Fifth Avenue, Clark Bar, Baby Ruth, Nestle Crunch, $100,000 Bar, KitKat, Butterfinger, Chunky, Twix.

VANILLA CANDY DISH ICE CREAM Add ½ cup small candies of your choice to the machine when the ice cream is semifrozen. Allow the machine to mix in the candy. Proceed with the recipe as directed. Candy suggestions include M&M's, Goobers, Raisinettes, Gummi Bears, Red Hots, Reese's Pieces, Skittles, Candy Corn, Jelly Beans, Junior Mints.

VANILLA CRACKER JACK ICE CREAM Add 1 cup crunchy caramel corn to the machine when the ice cream is semifrozen. Allow the machine to mix in the corn. Proceed with the recipe as directed.

VANILLA YOGURT ICE CREAM

A LARGE amount of vanilla is required to cut through the very tangy taste of yogurt in this ice cream.

2 cups plain yogurt

⅔ cup sugar

1½ cups light cream

2 tablespoons vanilla extract

Soak a large piece of cheesecloth or plain white paper towel in cold water. Squeeze out the water and line a colander or sieve with the wet cloth. Spoon the yogurt into the colander and set it into a larger bowl to catch the liquid that drains off from the yogurt. Place in the refrigerator and let drain for 2 or 3 hours. Approximately ⅔ cup of liquid will drain out.

Spoon the thickened yogurt into a large mixing bowl and whisk in the sugar. Stir until the sugar is completely dissolved, then add the cream and vanilla. Freeze in your ice cream machine according to the manufacturer's directions. When finished, the ice cream will be soft but ready to eat. For firmer ice cream, transfer to a freezer-safe container and freeze at least 2 hours.

◂ • ▸

Variations

DOUBLE YOGURT-RAISIN ICE CREAM Add ½ cup yogurt-covered raisins (available in health food stores) to the machine when the ice cream is semifrozen. Allow the machine to mix in the raisins. Proceed with the recipe as directed.

YOGURT BANANA CHIP ICE CREAM Add ½ cup chopped dried banana chips to the machine when the ice cream is semifrozen. Allow the machine to mix in the chips. Proceed with the recipe as directed.

YOGURT HONEY ICE CREAM Substitute honey for sugar. Proceed with the recipe as directed.

YOGURT PRETZEL CRUNCH ICE CREAM Add ½ cup white-chocolate-covered pretzel pieces to the machine when the ice cream is semifrozen. Allow the machine to mix in the pretzels. Proceed with the recipe as directed.

WHITE CHOCOLATE ICE CREAM

TRUE white chocolate contains cocoa butter, while white baking chips often contain palm oil or other fat. To ensure an authentic chocolate texture, use premium-quality white chocolate, often found in the candy section of your supermarket.

1 cup milk

2 large eggs

12 ounces white chocolate, chopped

1½ cups heavy cream

1 teaspoon vanilla extract

Bring the milk to a simmer in a heavy medium saucepan. Remove from the heat and slowly beat the hot milk into the eggs in a medium mixing bowl. Pour the entire mixture back into the pan and place over low heat. Stir constantly with a whisk or wooden spoon until the custard thickens slightly. Be careful not to let the mixture boil or the eggs will scramble. Remove from the heat and stir in the chocolate. Mix until the chocolate is melted. Pour the hot custard through a strainer into a large, clean bowl. Allow the custard to cool slightly, then stir in the cream and vanilla. Cover and refrigerate until cold or overnight.

Stir the chilled custard, then freeze in 1 or 2 batches in your ice cream machine according to the manufacturer's instructions. When finished, the ice cream will be soft but ready to eat. For firmer ice cream, transfer to a freezer-safe container and freeze at least 2 hours.

Variations

WHITE AND DARK CHOCOLATE ICE CREAM Add 1 cup shaved bittersweet chocolate to the machine when the ice cream is semifrozen. Allow the machine to mix in the chocolate. Proceed with the recipe as directed.

WHITE CHOCOLATE CHEESECAKE ICE CREAM Add 1 cup crumbled cheesecake (without crust) to the machine when the ice cream is semifrozen. Allow the machine to mix in the cake. Proceed with the recipe as directed.

continued

WHITE CHOCOLATE PEANUT CRUNCH ICE CREAM Add 1 cup crushed peanut brittle to the machine when the ice cream is semifrozen. Allow the machine to mix in the candy. Proceed with the recipe as directed.

WHITE CHOCOLATE RASPBERRY ALMOND CRUNCH ICE CREAM Stir 2 tablespoons water into ½ cup raspberry jam to loosen it up. Swirl the jam plus 2 tablespoons chopped toasted almonds (see page xvi) into the finished ice cream. Take care not to overswirl or the jam will "melt" into the ice cream. Streaks of jam should be visible. Serve immediately or freeze until firm.

WHITE CHOCOLATE STRAWBERRY ORANGE WAFER ICE CREAM Thinly slice 2 cups of strawberries and toss with 2 tablespoons sugar and 2 tablespoons orange liqueur. Allow the fruit to macerate for 2 hours. Add the fruit to the custard before freezing. Proceed with the recipe as directed, adding ½ cup crumbled sugar wafers to the machine when the ice cream is semifrozen. Allow the machine to mix in the wafers.

Sorbets and Granitas—
Sweet and Savory

APPLE SORBET

TART green apples are best for this sorbet. The color stays light green after freezing and the flavor is strong. Use the pulp as well as the juice to give the sorbet an applelike texture as well as flavor.

¾ cup sugar

1 cup clear unsweetened
    apple juice

4 green apples

Juice of 2 limes

Combine the sugar and apple juice in a small saucepan and place over low heat. Stir until the sugar dissolves and the syrup is clear. Remove from the heat and cool to room temperature.

Peel and core the apples. Roughly chop the fruit and place in a blender with the cool syrup and lime juice. Blend until completely smooth, about 1 minute. Freeze in 1 or 2 batches in your ice cream machine according to the manufacturer's instructions. When finished, the sorbet will be soft but ready to eat. For firmer sorbet, transfer to a freezer-safe container and freeze at least 2 hours.

‹ • ›

Variations

APPLE CHARDONNAY SORBET Substitute chardonnay wine for the apple juice. Proceed with the recipe as directed.

APPLE GINSENG SORBET Add 1 10ml vial ginseng extract to the blender along with the fruit. Proceed with the recipe as directed. (Check your health food store or call Whole xFoods (800-780-3663) for ginseng extract.)

APPLE THYME SORBET Add 1 teaspoon fresh thyme leaves to the blender along with the apples. Proceed with the recipe as directed.

SPICED APPLE SORBET Add ½ teaspoon ground cinnamon and ¼ teaspoon ground nutmeg to the blender along with the apples. Proceed with the recipe as directed.

BANANA SORBET

THIS is one of the few sorbet recipes that calls for milk and works with regular, low-fat, or even nonfat milk. The banana liqueur is optional, but helps bring out a stronger banana flavor.

2/3 cup sugar

1/2 cup water

2 tablespoons light corn syrup

1 cup milk

1 pound peeled bananas, broken into thirds (about 4 large bananas)

1 teaspoon vanilla extract

1/4 cup crème de banana liqueur or banana syrup (optional)

Combine the sugar, water, and corn syrup in a large saucepan. Place over medium heat and stir until the sugar dissolves. Raise the heat and boil without stirring, for 3 minutes. Turn off the heat and let the mixture cool slightly.

Add the milk and bananas to the sugar syrup. Return to a simmer and cook uncovered until the bananas are very soft and fragrant. This will take 5 to 10 minutes. The milk may look foamy.

Let the banana mixture cool slightly, then puree the bananas and syrup in a blender or a food processor. If necessary, do this in 2 or 3 batches. Stir in the vanilla and banana liqueur. Cover and refrigerate until cold or overnight.

Stir the chilled banana puree, then freeze in 1 or 2 batches in your ice cream machine according to the manufacturer's instructions. When finished, the sorbet will be soft but ready to eat. For firmer sorbet, transfer to a freezer-safe container and freeze at least 2 hours.

◂ • ▸

Variations

BANANA BLUEBERRY SORBET Soak 1/2 cup dried blueberries in 1/2 cup vodka or water for 1/2 hour. Add the blueberries with liquid to the sorbet mixture before freezing. Proceed with the recipe as directed.

BANANA COCONUT SORBET Substitute unsweetened coconut milk for the dairy milk and proceed with the recipe as directed.

BANANA DAIQUIRI SORBET Add ¼ cup gold rum and 2 tablespoons bottled sweetened lime juice before freezing. Proceed with the recipe as directed.

BANANA PINEAPPLE SORBET Substitute pineapple juice for the milk. Proceed with the recipe as directed.

"HOT" BANANA SORBET Add 1 teaspoon crushed red pepper flakes to the pan along with the bananas. Proceed with the recipe as directed.

BEET GRANITA

BEETS are very sweet, so very little sugar is needed to create this granita. It tastes like borscht and makes a wonderful start to any summer meal.

3 cups beet juice, fresh or bottled
¼ cup sugar

Combine the beet juice and sugar, stirring until the sugar completely dissolves. Refrigerate until cold. Freeze in 1 or 2 batches in your ice cream machine according to the manufacturer's directions. When finished, the granita will be soft and have the consistency of a sorbet. Transfer to a freezer-safe container and freeze to harden.

To serve, scrape the top of the granita with a heavy ice cream spade or scoop, creating shaved ice crystals. Serve in small, chilled dishes.

‹ • ›

Variations

GOLDEN BEET GRANITA Use golden beets to make the juice instead of red beets. Substitute 1 cup chardonnay for 1 cup of the beet juice. Proceed with the recipe as directed.

PINK RUSSIAN GRANITA Add ¼ cup sour cream or yogurt and ¼ cup vodka to the chilled beet mixture. Blend well and strain before freezing. Proceed with the recipe as directed.

SAVORY BEET GRANITA Add 1 teaspoon finely minced fresh marjoram or summer savory to the mixture before freezing. Proceed with the recipe as directed.

BLACKBERRY SORBET

MAKES ABOUT 3 CUPS

UNFORTUNATELY, fresh blackberries have a short growing period in the United States. Luckily, they freeze very well—simply lay them on a cookie sheet in the freezer until frozen, then place them in freezer bags.

½ cup water

¼ cup corn syrup

¼ cup sugar

3 cups blackberries

1 tablespoon fresh lime juice

3 tablespoons blackberry liqueur or syrup (optional)

Combine the water, corn syrup, and sugar in a small saucepan. Place over medium heat and stir until the sugar dissolves. Raise the heat and boil without stirring for 1 minute. Turn off the heat and let the mixture cool completely.

Place the sugar syrup, blackberries, lime juice, and liqueur in a blender. Process until the mixture is smooth. This will take about 30 seconds. If desired, pour the puree through a strainer to remove the seeds. Cover and refrigerate until cold.

Stir the chilled berry puree, then freeze in 1 or 2 batches in your ice cream machine according to the manufacturer's instructions. When finished, the sorbet will be soft but ready to eat. For firmer sorbet, transfer to a freezer-safe container and freeze at least 2 hours.

Variations

BLACKBERRY GINGER SORBET Add four 1-inch pieces of peeled fresh ginger to the pan along with the sugar. Remove the ginger after the syrup has cooled. Proceed with the recipe as directed.

BLACKBERRY LEMON SORBET Substitute the juice of 2 lemons for the lime juice. Add the grated zest of 1 lemon just before freezing. Proceed with the recipe as directed.

BLACKBERRY RHUBARB SORBET Add 1 cup sweetened rhubarb puree (see Rhubarb Ice Cream recipe, page 117) to the sorbet mixture before freezing. Proceed with the recipe as directed.

BLOOD ORANGE SORBET

BLOOD oranges earn their name from their dark red flesh. They are common throughout the Mediterranean region and are becoming readily available in the United States.

2/3 cup sugar

1 cup water

8 large blood oranges

Juice of 1 lime

Place the sugar and water in a small saucepan and set over low heat. Stir until the sugar dissolves and the syrup is clear. Remove from the heat and cool to room temperature.

To prepare the oranges, cut off the ends of the fruit so they sit flat on a cutting board. Then cut down the sides following the curve of the fruit, removing the rind and the white pith beneath. When the rind and pith are all removed, hold the fruit in one hand over a bowl and use a small paring knife in your other hand to cut between the membranes, letting the clean orange sections fall into the bowl. Be careful not to cut down into your hand! When all the sections are cut away, squeeze the remaining fruit pulp in your hand to extract any residual juice. Pour the orange segments and juice into a blender and blend for 10 seconds to chop up the fruit. You should have about 2 cups of juice and pulp. Combine the orange puree, cooled sugar syrup, and lime juice. Cover and refrigerate until cold.

Stir the chilled mixture, then freeze in 1 or 2 batches in your ice cream machine according to the manufacturer's instructions. When finished, the sorbet will be soft but ready to eat. For firmer sorbet, transfer to a freezer-safe container and freeze at least 2 hours.

◄ • ►

Variations

BLOOD ORANGE CAMPARI SORBET Add ½ cup Campari to the blender along with the fruit. Proceed with the recipe as directed.

BLOOD ORANGE CHERRY SORBET Add ½ cup pitted sweet cherries to the blender along with the oranges. Blend until the fruit is pureed, about 30 seconds. Proceed with the recipe as directed.

BLOOD ORANGE PINEAPPLE SORBET Add 1 cup crushed pineapple in heavy syrup to the blender along with the oranges. Blend until the fruit is pureed, about 30 seconds. Proceed with the recipe as directed.

CHOCOLATE BLOOD ORANGE SORBET Swirl ½ cup chocolate syrup or chocolate sauce into the finished sorbet. Be careful not to overswirl or the chocolate will "melt" into the sorbet. Streaks of chocolate should be visible. Serve immediately or freeze until firm.

MOROCCAN BLOOD ORANGE SORBET Add ½ teaspoon ground cumin and ½ teaspoon ground cinnamon to the blender along with the fruit. Proceed with the recipe as directed.

BLUEBERRY SORBET

Either fresh blueberries or frozen work well in this recipe. Just remember to measure the volume of your frozen berries before you defrost them, or use their weight as a guide for even better accuracy.

⅔ cup sugar

⅓ cup water

1 heaping quart
  blueberries, about
    1¼ pounds

Juice of ½ lime

Combine the sugar and water in a small saucepan and place over low heat. Stir until the sugar dissolves and the syrup is clear. Remove from heat and cool to room temperature.

Place the blueberries in a blender with the cool syrup and lime juice. Blend until completely smooth, about 30 seconds. Freeze in 1 or 2 batches in your ice cream machine according to the manufacturer's instructions. When finished, the sorbet will be soft but ready to eat. For firmer sorbet, transfer to a freezer-safe container and freeze at least 2 hours.

◂ • ▸

Variations

BLUEBERRY APRICOT SORBET Add 1 cup canned apricots in heavy syrup to the blender along with the blueberries. If necessary, puree the fruit in 2 or 3 batches. Optional: add 2 tablespoons apricot brandy before freezing. Proceed with the recipe as directed.

BLUEBERRY COCONUT SORBET Substitute coconut water (see page 154) for the water. Proceed with the recipe as directed.

BLUEBERRY PEACH SORBET Add 1 large peach, pitted but unpeeled, to the blender along with the blueberries. Add 2 additional tablespoons sugar. If necessary, puree the fruit in 2 or 3 batches. Optional: add 2 tablespoons peach schnapps before freezing. Proceed with the recipe as directed.

CANTALOUPE SORBET

A FRESH, sweet melon is the only kind of melon that transforms into a fine sorbet, so this dessert can be made only in the summer, unless you are lucky enough to live where fresh melons are available year-round.

1 small ripe cantaloupe or muskmelon
¼ cup orange juice
¾ cup superfine sugar
½ teaspoon salt

Remove the rind and seeds from the melon. Cut the flesh into ½-inch cubes. You should have about 2 heaping cups of fruit. Place the cut-up melon in a blender with the orange juice, sugar, and salt. Blend until the melon is pureed and the sugar has dissolved, about 30 seconds. Cover and refrigerate until cold.

Stir the chilled mixture, then freeze in 1 or 2 batches in your ice cream machine according to the manufacturer's instructions. When finished, the sorbet will be soft but ready to eat. For firmer sorbet, transfer to a freezer-safe container and freeze at least 2 hours.

◄ • ►

Variations

CANTALOUPE BASIL SORBET Add 4 large fresh basil leaves to the blender along with the fruit. Proceed with the recipe as directed.

CANTALOUPE BLUEBERRY SORBET Add 1 cup fresh blueberries and 3 tablespoons additional sugar to the blender along with the cantaloupe. If necessary, puree fruit in 2 or 3 batches. Proceed with the recipe as directed.

CANTALOUPE STRAWBERRY SORBET Add 1 cup sliced fresh strawberries and 2 tablespoons honey to the blender along with the cantaloupe. If necessary, puree fruit in 2 or 3 batches. Proceed with the recipe as directed.

MIXED MELON SORBET Substitute any combination of melons you like: honeydew, crenshaw, casaba, or watermelon. Just be sure to use 2 heaping cups of chopped fruit. Proceed with the recipe as directed.

CARROT GRANITA

THIS granita can be made from fresh or bottled carrot juice, available in your supermarket's produce section or at any health food store.

3 cups carrot juice, fresh or
bottled

¼ cup light brown sugar

Combine the carrot juice and brown sugar, stirring until the sugar is completely dissolved. Refrigerate until cold. Freeze in 1 or 2 batches in your ice cream machine according to the manufacturer's directions. When finished, the granita will be soft and have the consistency of a sorbet. Transfer to a freezer-safe container and freeze to harden.

To serve, scrape the top of the granita with a heavy ice cream spade or scoop, to create shaved ice crystals. Serve in small chilled dishes.

◂ • ▸

Variations

CARROT APPLE GRANITA Substitute 1½ cups clear apple juice for 1½ cups of the carrot juice. Proceed with the recipe as directed.

CARROT CRANBERRY GRANITA Substitute 1½ cups cranberry juice for 1½ cups of the carrot juice. Proceed with the recipe as directed.

CARROT FIRE GRANITA Add 2 teaspoons Tabasco sauce to the carrot juice before freezing. Proceed with the recipe as directed.

CHOCOLATE SORBET #1 (DARK AND DENSE)

THIS sorbet is so dense, rich, and intense, it's hard to believe it's made without cream or cocoa butter.

2 cups water

1 cup sugar

1 cup unsweetened cocoa powder

Combine the water and sugar in a heavy saucepan and place over medium heat. Stir until the sugar dissolves. Whisk in the cocoa and bring the mixture to a simmer. Simmer for 3 minutes, stirring constantly.

Remove from the heat and pour through a fine strainer into a bowl. Chill in the refrigerator for 2 hours. Stir the cool mixture, then freeze in 1 or 2 batches in your ice cream machine according to the manufacturer's instructions.

When finished, the sorbet will be soft but ready to eat. For firmer sorbet, transfer to a freezer-safe container and freeze at least 2 hours.

◄ • ►

Variations

CHOCOLATE ESPRESSO SORBET Add 1 teaspoon instant espresso powder along with the cocoa powder. Proceed with the recipe as directed.

CHOCOLATE MINT SORBET Add ½ teaspoon peppermint extract to the cooled mixture before freezing. Proceed with the recipe as directed.

CHOCOLATE NUT SORBET Add ½ cup chopped toasted pecans or almonds (see page xvi) to the machine when the sorbet is semifrozen. Allow the machine to mix in the nuts. Proceed with the recipe as directed.

CHOCOLATE SOUFFLÉ SORBET Swirl 1 cup of marshmallow creme into the finished sorbet. Be careful not to overswirl or the marshmallow will "melt" into the sorbet. Streaks of marshmallow should be visible. Serve immediately or freeze until firm.

CHOCOLATE SORBET #2 (RICH AND CREAMY)

THE cocoa butter in the chocolate makes this sorbet almost as rich as ice cream.

3 cups water

1¼ cups sugar

3 tablespoons light corn syrup

⅔ cup unsweetened cocoa powder

2 ounces semisweet chocolate

1 tablespoon vanilla extract

Combine the water, sugar, and corn syrup in a heavy saucepan. Place over low heat and stir until the sugar dissolves. Raise the heat to medium, bring to a boil, and cook 2 minutes. Reduce the heat to low. Whisk in the cocoa and simmer 2 minutes more. Remove from heat. Add the chocolate and stir until it's completely melted and the mixture is smooth. Cool to room temperature. Stir in the vanilla. Cover and chill for at least 1 hour.

Stir the cooled mixture, then freeze in 1 or 2 batches in your ice cream machine according to the manufacturer's instructions. When finished, the sorbet will be soft but ready to eat. For firmer sorbet, transfer to a freezer-safe container and freeze at least 2 hours.

◂ • ▸

Variations

CHOCOLATE CHERRY SORBET Add ½ cup dried cherries to the machine when the sorbet is semifrozen. Allow the machine to mix in the cherries. Proceed with the recipe as directed.

CHOCOLATE CHIP SORBET Add ½ cup miniature chocolate chips to the machine when the sorbet is semifrozen. Allow the machine to mix in the chips. Proceed with the recipe as directed.

CHOCOLATE COCONUT SORBET Substitute 1½ cups unsweetened coconut milk for 1½ cups of the water. Proceed with the recipe as directed.

MEXICAN CHOCOLATE SORBET Add ¼ teaspoon almond extract and ½ teaspoon ground cinnamon to the pan along with the cocoa. Proceed with the recipe as directed.

CIDER SORBET

FRESHLY pressed apple cider makes the best sorbet. If you can't find it, use any unsweetened apple cider or apple juice.

3 cups fresh apple cider
1½ cups sugar
Juice of 1 lemon

Bring the cider to a simmer in a medium saucepan. Add the sugar and stir until it is completely dissolved. Remove from the heat and pour the cider into a jar or bowl. Refrigerate until cold or overnight.

Stir in the lemon juice, then freeze in 1 or 2 batches in your ice cream machine according to the manufacturer's instructions. When finished, the sorbet will be soft but ready to eat. For firmer sorbet, transfer to a freezer-safe container and freeze at least 2 hours.

◂ • • ▸

Variations

CIDER COMFORT SORBET Add ½ cup Southern Comfort before freezing. Proceed with the recipe as directed.

CRANBERRY CIDER SORBET Substitute 1½ cups cranberry juice for 1½ cups of the cider. Proceed with the recipe as directed.

LEMONGRASS CIDER SORBET Slice a 6-inch piece of fresh lemongrass into 1-inch pieces. Add to the pan along with the sugar. Proceed with the recipe as directed, removing the lemongrass before freezing.

MAPLE CIDER SORBET Substitute ½ cup maple syrup for ½ cup of the sugar. Proceed with the recipe as directed.

SPICED CIDER SORBET Add 1 teaspoon grated fresh orange zest and ½ teaspoon ground cinnamon to the pan along with the sugar. Proceed with the recipe as directed.

COCONUT SORBET

RIPE coconuts are filled with a fragrant, clear liquid called coconut water, sold in some markets and specialty food stores. Coconut milk, on the other hand, is made by steeping shredded coconut in boiling water, which releases the flavor from the coconut meat. Luckily, both coconut milk and coconut water can be found in cans, making this a very easy sorbet to prepare.

1 cup coconut water

¾ cup sugar

2 cups unsweetened
coconut milk

Combine the coconut water and sugar in a small saucepan. Place over low heat and stir until the sugar dissolves. Allow the syrup to cool completely. Stir in the coconut milk. Cover and refrigerate until cold.

Stir the chilled mixture, then freeze in 1 or 2 batches in your ice cream machine according to the manufacturer's instructions. When finished, the sorbet will be soft but ready to eat. For firmer sorbet, transfer to a freezer-safe container and freeze at least 2 hours.

Variations

COCONUT ALMOND SORBET Add ¼ teaspoon almond extract along with the coconut milk. Proceed with the recipe as directed.

COCONUT LIME SORBET Increase the sugar to 1 cup. Proceed with the recipe as directed, adding ¼ cup freshly squeezed lime juice along with the coconut milk.

COCONUT RUM SORBET Add ½ cup coconut-flavored rum along with the coconut milk. Proceed with the recipe as directed.

COFFEE GRANITA

USE freshly brewed espresso or extra-strong coffee to make this granita. If you don't have fresh coffee beans, use instant espresso or instant coffee, using twice as much coffee crystals as indicated on the jar.

¾ cup sugar

1½ cups water

2½ cups strong coffee

¼ cup coffee liqueur
(optional)

Combine the sugar and water in a small, heavy saucepan. Place over medium heat and stir until the sugar is completely dissolved. Boil the syrup for 5 minutes, then remove from the heat. Add the coffee and liqueur. Refrigerate until cold or overnight.

Freeze in 1 or 2 batches in your ice cream machine according to the manufacturer's directions. When finished, the granita will be soft and have the consistency of a sorbet. Transfer to a freezer-safe container and freeze to harden. To serve, scrape the top of the granita with a heavy ice cream spade or scoop, creating ice crystals. Serve in small, chilled dishes.

Alternately, pour the coffee mixture into ice cube trays, filling only half way, and freeze until firm. Before serving, process the coffee ice cubes in a food processor until chopped and slushy. Serve immediately.

‹ • ›

Variations

HAZELNUT COFFEE GRANITA Add ¼ cup hazelnut syrup or liqueur before freezing. Proceed with the recipe as directed.

RASPBERRY COFFEE GRANITA Add ¼ cup raspberry syrup or liqueur before freezing. Proceed with the recipe as directed.

VANILLA COFFEE GRANITA Split a vanilla bean open lengthwise and scrape out the seeds. Add the bean and seeds to the pan along with the sugar. Proceed with the recipe as directed, removing the vanilla bean before freezing.

CRANBERRY SORBET

TRY this tart sorbet as a palate cleanser between the corn chowder and the roast turkey next Thanksgiving.

½ pound fresh cranberries
(about 2 cups)

1 cup plus 2 tablespoons
sugar

1½ cups red wine or
cranberry juice

1 cup water

¼ teaspoon salt

Place the cranberries, sugar, wine, water, and salt in a large heavy saucepan. Stir over medium heat until the sugar is dissolved and the mixture comes to a simmer. Continue to cook for 2 minutes or until the cranberries pop and begin to soften. Remove from the heat and allow the cranberry mixture to cool slightly.

Puree in a blender. If necessary, do this in 2 batches. Pass the puree through a food mill to remove the skins. You may use a strainer, but the puree will be thick and will need to be rubbed through, using a large wooden spoon. Cover and refrigerate until cold or overnight.

Stir the chilled mixture, then freeze in 1 or 2 batches in your ice cream machine according to the manufacturer's instructions. When finished, the sorbet will be soft but ready to eat. For firmer sorbet, transfer to a freezer-safe container and freeze at least 2 hours.

◄ • ►

Variations

CRANBERRY GINGER SORBET Substitute white wine or apple juice for the red wine. Add 1 tablespoon grated fresh ginger to the pan along with the sugar. Proceed with the recipe as directed.

CRANBERRY ORANGE SORBET Substitute orange juice for the wine. Add 1 tablespoon grated orange zest before freezing. Proceed with the recipe as directed.

CRANBERRY PINEAPPLE SORBET Substitute unsweetened pineapple juice for the wine. Proceed with the recipe as directed.

SEA BREEZE SORBET Substitute grapefruit juice for the wine. Proceed with the recipe as directed, adding ½ cup vodka before freezing, if desired.

SPICED CRANBERRY SORBET Add ½ teaspoon ground cinnamon, ¼ teaspoon ground cloves, and 1 teaspoon grated fresh lemon zest along with the salt. Proceed with the recipe as directed.

CUCUMBER GRANITA

TRY this light, refreshing, and unusual ice as a summer lunch opener, served in a hollowed-out tomato. Drizzle this granita with a little buttermilk for a very interesting summer "soup."

4 large cucumbers

¼ cup sugar

3 tablespoons chopped fresh dill

¼ teaspoon salt

Peel the cucumbers, slice them in half lengthwise, and scoop out the seeds with a spoon. Roughly chop the cucumbers and place in a food processor with the sugar, dill, and salt. Process until completely smooth, stopping to scrape down the sides of the work bowl as necessary. Refrigerate until cold or overnight.

Stir the chilled mixture, then freeze in 1 or 2 batches in your ice cream machine according to the manufacturer's directions. When finished, the granita will be soft and have the consistency of a sorbet. Transfer to a freezer-safe container and freeze to harden. To serve, scrape the top of the granita with a heavy ice cream spade or scoop, creating shaved ice crystals. Serve in small, chilled dishes.

Alternately, pour the cucumber mixture into ice cube trays, filling only half way, and freeze until firm. Before serving, process the cucumber ice cubes in a food processor until chopped and slushy. Serve immediately.

◄ • ▶

Variations

CRACKED CUCUMBER GRANITA Substitute 1 tablespoon cracked black peppercorns for the dill. Proceed with the recipe as directed.

CUCUMBER BASIL GRANITA Omit the dill. Add 8 fresh basil leaves to the food processor along with the cucumber. Proceed with the recipe as directed.

CUCUMBER MINT GRANITA Omit the dill. Add 1 teaspoon fresh mint leaves to the food processor along with the cucumber. Proceed with the recipe as directed. Optional: add 1 tablespoon green crème de menthe before freezing.

CUCUMBER THYME GRANITA Substitute 2 teaspoons fresh thyme leaves for the dill. Proceed with the recipe as directed.

GRAPEFRUIT SORBET

MAKES ABOUT 1 QUART

WHITE grapefruits can be very tart; pink ones a little sweeter; and ruby reds, sweet as sugar. Let your taste be your guide.

2 large grapefruits

⅔ cup sugar

3 tablespoons water

2 large egg whites

To prepare the grapefruits, cut off the ends of the fruit so they sit flat on a cutting board. Then cut down the sides following the curve of the fruit, removing the rind and the white pith beneath. When the rind and pith are all removed, hold the fruit in one hand over a bowl and use a small paring knife, in your other hand, to cut between the membranes, letting the clean grapefruit sections fall into the bowl. Take care not to cut through to your hand! When all the sections are cut away, squeeze the remaining fruit pulp in your hand to remove any residual juice. Pour the grapefruit segments and juice into a blender and blend for 10 seconds to chop up the fruit. Set aside.

Combine the sugar and water in a small saucepan and place over low heat. Stir until the sugar dissolves. Raise the heat and boil the syrup for 1 minute, then remove from the heat. Lightly beat the egg whites with a whisk or an electric beater until foamy, about 10 seconds. Slowly beat in the hot sugar syrup. Continue to beat until the meringue cools down slightly. Add the grapefruit juice and pulp. Cover and refrigerate until cold or overnight. The mixture may separate, leaving foam on top, but it will incorporate into the sorbet when it freezes.

Stir the chilled mixture, then freeze in 1 or 2 batches in your ice cream machine according to the manufacturer's instructions. When finished, the sorbet will be soft but ready to eat. For firmer sorbet, transfer to a freezer-safe container and freeze at least 2 hours.

◂ • ▸

Variations

GRAPEFRUIT CAMPARI SORBET Add ½ cup Campari to the blender along with the fruit. Proceed with the recipe as directed.

GRAPEFRUIT GINSENG SORBET Add one 10ml vial ginseng extract to the blender along with the fruit. Proceed with the recipe as directed. For ginseng extract, check your local health food store or call Whole Foods (800-780-3663).

GRAPEFRUIT KIWI SORBET Add 2 small peeled and quartered kiwis to the blender along with the grapefruit. Process until the fruit is pureed, about 30 seconds. Proceed with the recipe as directed.

GRAPEFRUIT POBLANO SORBET Add ½ cup chopped roasted poblano chiles to the blender along with the grapefruit. Proceed with the recipe as directed. Note: to roast poblano chiles, place the chiles under the broiler, turning often, until the skin is charred all over. Place the charred chiles in a paper bag, seal, and let rest for 15 minutes. The skins should now peel off easily. Split the chiles open and discard the seeds.

GRAPEFRUIT TARRAGON SORBET Add 2 tablespoons chopped fresh tarragon leaves to the blender along with the grapefruit. Proceed with the recipe as directed.

GREENGAGE PLUM SORBET

GREENGAGE plums are small and green, but turn brown quickly once they are cut open. Add the lime juice immediately and freeze the mixture without delay to help this sorbet retain its gemlike color.

½ cup sugar

½ cup water

2 tablespoons light corn syrup

1 pound greengage plums

Juice of 2 medium limes (about 3 tablespoons)

¼ teaspoon salt

Combine the sugar, water, and corn syrup in a small saucepan. Place over medium heat and stir until the sugar dissolves. Bring to a boil and cook without stirring for 3 minutes. Remove from heat and cool to room temperature.

Pit the plums and cut them in half. Place the plums in a blender or food processor with the lime juice, salt, and cool sugar syrup. Process until the mixture is smooth, about 30 seconds. If the puree is too thick to blend properly, add additional water 1 tablespoon at a time until the mixture blends easily. To avoid any discoloration, freeze immediately in 1 or 2 batches in your ice cream machine according to the manufacturer's instructions. When finished, the sorbet will be soft but ready to eat. For firmer sorbet, transfer to a freezer-safe container and freeze at least 2 hours.

‹ • ›

Variations

DOUBLE PLUM WINE SORBET Add ½ cup sweet plum wine before freezing. Proceed with the recipe as directed.

GREENGAGE GRAPE SORBET Substitute ½ pound seedless green grapes for ½ pound of the greengage plums. Proceed with the recipe as directed.

GREENGAGE RIESLING SORBET Add ½ cup Riesling wine or other sweet white wine before freezing. Proceed with the recipe as directed.

GREENGAGE SAKE SORBET Add ½ cup sake (Japanese rice wine) before freezing. Proceed with the recipe as directed.

HONEYDEW SORBET

HONEYDEW is very sweet and fragrant, but the flavor is subtle. The addition of melon liqueur helps bring out the flavor of even the sweetest, ripest melon.

1 small honeydew melon

¼ cup white grape juice

¾ cup superfine sugar

2 tablespoons melon
  liqueur or syrup

½ teaspoon salt

Remove the rind and seeds from the melon. Cut the flesh into ½-inch cubes. You should have about 2 heaping cups of fruit. Place the cut-up melon in a blender with the grape juice, sugar, liqueur, and salt. Blend until the melon is pureed and the sugar has dissolved, about 30 seconds. Cover and refrigerate until cold.

Stir the chilled mixture, then freeze in 1 or 2 batches in your ice cream machine according to the manufacturer's instructions. When finished, the sorbet will be soft but ready to eat. For firmer sorbet, transfer to a freezer-safe container and freeze at least 2 hours.

‹ • • ›

Variations

HONEYDEW HONEY SORBET Substitute honey for some or all of the sugar, depending on your taste. Proceed with the recipe as directed.

HONEYDEW LEMON DROP SORBET Add ½ cup vodka and the grated zest of 1 lemon to the blender along with the fruit. Proceed with the recipe as directed.

HONEYDEW TARRAGON SORBET Add 1 tablespoon chopped fresh tarragon leaves to the blender along with the fruit. Proceed with the recipe as directed.

KIWI SORBET

MAKES ABOUT 1 QUART

KIWI can vary in size, so it's best to weigh them in the store. Choose fruit that gives a little when gently squeezed. If they are too hard, they may be too sour.

3/4 cup plus 2 tablespoons sugar

3/4 cup water

1 1/2 pounds ripe kiwis (6 to 8 medium size)

Juice of 1 lime

1/2 teaspoon vanilla extract

Combine the sugar and water in a small saucepan and place over low heat. Stir until the sugar dissolves. Raise the heat and boil the syrup for 1 minute. Remove from the heat and allow the syrup to cool to room temperature.

Peel the kiwis and cut into quarters. Place the fruit in a blender with the cool syrup, lime juice, and vanilla. Blend on low until the mixture is smooth, about 1 minute. Refrigerate until cold or overnight.

Stir the chilled mixture, then freeze in 1 or 2 batches in your ice cream machine according to the manufacturer's instructions. When finished, the sorbet will be soft but ready to eat. For firmer sorbet, transfer to a freezer-safe container and freeze at least 2 hours.

Variations

KIWI BANANA SORBET Substitute 1 large banana, thinly sliced, for 1/2 of the kiwis. Proceed with the recipe as directed.

KIWI COCKTAIL SORBET Omit the vanilla. Add 1/2 cup gold rum or coconut-flavored rum before freezing. Proceed with the recipe as directed.

KIWI STRAWBERRY SORBET Substitute 1 cup sliced fresh strawberries for half of the kiwis. Proceed with the recipe as directed.

KUMQUAT SORBET

KUMQUATS look like tiny oranges; however, they are quite bitter. You can eat them rind and all, but you must cook them to soften the rind before using them for sorbet.

1 quart kumquats
(about ¾ pound)
1½ cups water
1 cup sugar

Simmer the kumquats in the water over low heat for 5 minutes. Remove the fruit from the water with a slotted spoon and set aside. Add the sugar to the water and stir until dissolved. Raise the heat to medium and boil the syrup for 3 minutes. Return the kumquats to the boiling syrup and immediately remove from heat. Allow the fruit to cool in the syrup. When completely cool, puree the fruit and syrup by passing it through a food mill. Refrigerate until cold or overnight.

Stir the chilled mixture, then freeze in 1 or 2 batches in your ice cream machine according to the manufacturer's instructions. When finished, the sorbet will be soft but ready to eat. For firmer sorbet, transfer to a freezer-safe container and freeze at least 2 hours.

◄ • ►

Variations

KUMQUAT FENNEL SORBET Add 2 teaspoons whole fennel seeds to the pan along with the sugar. Proceed with the recipe as directed.

KUMQUAT TONIC SORBET Add ½ cup tonic water before freezing. Proceed with the recipe as directed. Optional: add ¼ cup gin along with the tonic.

LEMON SORBET

FRESHLY squeezed lemon juice gives this sorbet a flavor that's reminiscent of homemade lemonade: tart yet very refreshing.

1½ cups sugar

2 cups water

1 large egg white

¾ cup fresh lemon juice, about 4 lemons

Combine the sugar and water in a small saucepan and place over low heat. Stir until the sugar dissolves completely. Raise the heat and boil the syrup 1 minute. Remove from the heat.

In a mixing bowl, lightly beat the egg white with a whisk or an electric beater until foamy, about 10 seconds. Slowly beat in the hot sugar syrup. Continue to beat until the meringue cools down slightly. Add the lemon juice. Cover and refrigerate until cold or overnight. The mixture will have foam on top, but it will incorporate into the sorbet when it freezes.

Stir the chilled mixture, then freeze in 1 or 2 batches in your ice cream machine according to the manufacturer's instructions. When finished, the sorbet will be soft but ready to eat. For firmer sorbet, transfer to a freezer-safe container and freeze at least 2 hours.

◂ • ▸

Variations

LEMON BALM SORBET Add 2 tablespoons minced fresh lemon balm before freezing. Proceed with the recipe as directed.

LEMON DROP SORBET Add ½ cup lemon-flavored vodka before freezing. Proceed with the recipe as directed.

LEMON VERBENA SORBET Substitute brewed lemon verbena tea for the water. Proceed with the recipe as directed.

RASPBERRY LEMON SORBET Add 1 cup fresh raspberries to the sugar syrup just before beating into the egg whites. Proceed with the recipe as directed.

LIME SORBET

To help get all the juice out, cut the limes in half and stab the cut side with a fork while squeezing them.

1¼ cups sugar

2 cups water

1 large egg white

⅔ cup fresh lime juice

   (from 6 or 7 large limes)

Combine the sugar and water in a small saucepan and place over low heat. Stir until the sugar dissolves completely. Raise the heat and boil the syrup 1 minute. Remove from the heat.

In a medium mixing bowl, lightly beat the egg white with a whisk or an electric beater until foamy, about 10 seconds. Slowly beat in the hot sugar syrup. Continue to beat until the meringue cools down slightly. Add the lime juice. Cover and refrigerate until cold or overnight. The mixture will have foam on top, but will incorporate into the sorbet when it freezes.

Stir the chilled mixture, then freeze in your ice cream machine according to the manufacturer's instructions. When finished, the sorbet will be soft but ready to eat. For firmer sorbet, transfer to a freezer-safe container and freeze at least 2 hours.

‹ • ›

Variations

COCONUT LIME SORBET Substitute coconut water for the water (see page 154). Proceed with the recipe as directed.

DAIQUIRI SORBET Add ½ cup white rum before freezing. Proceed with the recipe as directed.

KEY LIME SORBET Substitute key lime juice for the regular lime juice. Proceed with the recipe as directed.

MARGARITA SORBET Add ¼ cup tequila and ¼ cup orange liqueur before freezing. Continue with the recipe as directed.

LYCHEE SORBET

Canned lychees are available in many supermarkets or almost any Asian grocery. If you can't find them, stop by your local Chinese restaurant and ask them to sell you a quart or two to go.

two 20-ounce cans lychees
in heavy syrup

½ cup sugar

¼ cup water

2 large egg whites, lightly
beaten

Drain the lychees, reserving the syrup. Puree the lychees with ½ cup reserved syrup in a blender or food processor until smooth, about 20 seconds. Pour through a sieve, scraping with a whisk or wooden spoon to push as much of the fruit through as you can. Set aside.

Combine the sugar and water in a small saucepan and place over low heat. Stir until the sugar dissolves completely. Raise heat and boil the syrup 1 minute. Remove from the heat.

In a medium mixing bowl, lightly beat the egg white with a whisk or an electric beater until foamy, about 10 seconds. Slowly beat in the hot sugar syrup. Continue to beat until the meringue cools down slightly. Add the lychee puree. Cover and refrigerate until cold or overnight. The mixture will have foam on top, but will incorporate into the sorbet when it freezes.

Stir the chilled mixture, then freeze in your ice cream machine according to the manufacturer's instructions. When finished, the sorbet will be soft but ready to eat. For firmer sorbet, transfer to a freezer-safe container and freeze at least 2 hours.

‹ • ›

Variations

LYCHEE APPLE SORBET Omit the lychee canning syrup. Substitute apple juice concentrate for the water. Proceed with the recipe as directed, boiling the sugar syrup for only 30 seconds.

LYCHEE FLOWER SORBET Add 1 tablespoon rose water or orange flower water to the cooled sorbet mixture. Proceed with the recipe as directed.

continued

LYCHEE GINGER SORBET Add ¼ cup minced crystallized ginger to the machine when the sorbet is semifrozen. Allow the machine to mix in the ginger. Proceed with the recipe as directed.

LYCHEE MELON SORBET Use only 1 can of lychees. Add 1 heaping cup chopped honeydew melon to the blender or food processor along with the remaining lychees. Proceed with the recipe as directed. Optional: add 2 tablespoons melon liqueur before freezing.

LYCHEE SOUR CHERRY SORBET Substitute sour cherry syrup for heavy syrup. Proceed with the recipe as directed.

MANGO SORBET

MANGOES should feel heavy in your hand, give slightly when pressed, and smell fragrant.

1 cup sugar

¾ cup water

2 ripe mangoes, about
  ½ pound each

Juice of 1 lime

Combine the sugar and water in a small saucepan and place over low heat. Stir until the sugar dissolves completely and the syrup is clear. Remove from the heat and allow to cool to room temperature.

Peel the mangoes and cut as much of the fruit as you can away from the large pits. If the mangoes are very ripe and juicy, and you feel adventurous, squeeze the pulp and juice off the pits with your hands. It's messy work, so do it over a large bowl.

Combine the cooled syrup, mango pulp, and lime juice in a blender or food processor. Blend until completely smooth, about 30 seconds. Cover and refrigerate until cold or overnight.

Stir the chilled mixture, then freeze in your ice cream machine according to the manufacturer's instructions. When finished, the sorbet will be soft but ready to eat. For firmer sorbet, transfer to a freezer-safe container and freeze at least 2 hours.

◂ • ▸

Variations

MANGO MINT SORBET Add 10 to 12 fresh mint leaves to the blender along with the mangoes. Proceed with the recipe as directed.

MANGO ORANGE SORBET Add ¼ cup orange juice concentrate to the blender along with the mangoes. Proceed with the recipe as directed.

MANGO PASSION SORBET Add ¼ cup passion fruit concentrate to the blender along with the mangoes. Proceed with the recipe as directed.

PAPAYA SORBET

FOR a great deal on papayas, head directly to Chinatown or your local Asian grocery. The fruit is usually cheaper, riper, and available all year long.

---

2 small ripe papayas,
    about 1 pound each

Juice of 2 limes

⅓ cup sugar

⅓ cup light corn syrup

½ cup water

½ teaspoon salt

2 teaspoons grenadine
    (optional)

Cut the papayas in half and scoop out the seeds with a spoon. Peel the papayas with a small paring knife. Cut the fruit into small pieces, about ½ inch. Place the fruit in a blender with the lime juice, sugar, corn syrup, water, salt, and grenadine. Blend for 30 seconds or until the mixture is smooth. Cover and refrigerate until cold or overnight.

Stir the chilled mixture, then freeze in your ice cream machine according to the manufacturer's instructions. When finished, the sorbet will be soft but ready to eat. For firmer sorbet, transfer to a freezer-safe container and freeze at least 2 hours.

◄ • ►

Variations

HAWAIIAN PAPAYA SORBET Add ½ cup macadamia nuts to the blender along with the papayas. Blend until the mixture is smooth, about 1 minute. Proceed with the recipe as directed.

PAPAYA BERRY SORBET Increase the sugar to ½ cup. Add 1 cup fresh berries of your choice to the blender along with the papayas. Proceed with the recipe as directed.

PAPAYA MANGO SORBET Add the pulp of 1 small mango to the blender along with the papayas. Proceed with the recipe as directed.

PEACH SORBET

To peel or not to peel, that is the dilemma. Without the peel, the sorbet is smooth and pure yellow. With the peel, the sorbet has a little more texture and tiny pink flecks that make it very pretty.

½ cup sugar

½ cup water

¼ cup light corn syrup

1½ pounds fresh sweet
 peaches, pitted and
 sliced

Juice of 1 lemon

¼ teaspoon salt

Combine the sugar, water, and corn syrup in a small saucepan. Place over medium heat and stir until the sugar dissolves. Boil without stirring for 1 minute. Remove from the heat and cool to room temperature.

Place the peaches in a blender or food processor along with the lemon juice, salt, and cool sugar syrup. Process until the mixture is smooth, about 30 seconds. If the puree is too thick to blend properly, add additional water 1 tablespoon at a time until the mixture blends easily.

Freeze immediately in your ice cream machine according to the manufacturer's instructions. When finished, the sorbet will be soft but ready to eat. For firmer sorbet, transfer to a freezer-safe container and freeze at least 2 hours.

◄ • ▸

Variations

PEACHCOT SORBET Substitute ¾ pound unpeeled apricots for ¾ pound of the peaches. Proceed with the recipe as directed. Optional: add 2 tablespoons apricot brandy before freezing.

PEACH MELBA SORBET Increase the sugar to ¾ cup. Add 1 cup fresh raspberries to the blender along with the peaches. If necessary, puree the fruit in 1 or 2 batches. Proceed with the recipe as directed.

continued

PEACH THYME SORBET Add 2 teaspoons chopped fresh thyme leaves to the blender along with the peaches. Proceed the with recipe as directed.

PEACHY ALMOND SORBET Add ½ cup amaretto liqueur to the sorbet mixture before blending. Proceed with the recipe as directed.

PEAR SORBET

ANY variety of fresh pear will work for this sorbet. Choose pears that are fragrant and slightly soft. In fact, the softer the pear, the better—as long (of course) as it's not rotten.

¾ cup plus 1 tablespoon
   sugar

⅔ cup water

1½ pounds ripe pears
   (3 or 4 medium)

Juice of 1 lemon

½ teaspoon salt

Combine the sugar and water in a small saucepan and place over low heat. Stir until the sugar dissolves completely. Raise the heat and boil the syrup 1 minute. Remove from the heat and allow the syrup to cool to room temperature.

Peel the pears and remove the cores. Cut the pears into small pieces and place in a blender with the cooled sugar syrup, lemon juice, and salt. Blend on low until the mixture is smooth. Refrigerate for at least 1 hour.

Stir the chilled mixture, then freeze in your ice cream machine according to the manufacturer's instructions. When finished, the sorbet will be soft but ready to eat. For firmer sorbet, transfer to a freezer-safe container and freeze at least 2 hours.

◂ • ▸

Variations

CABERNET PEAR SORBET Substitute a hearty red wine (like cabernet or zinfandel) for the water. Proceed with the recipe as directed.

LEMON PEAR SORBET Increase the lemon juice to ¼ cup. Add the grated zest of 1 lemon to the blender along with the pears. Proceed with the recipe as directed.

PEAR GINSENG SORBET Add one 10ml vial of ginseng extract to the blender along with the pears. Proceed with the recipe as directed. Check your local health food store for ginseng extract or call Whole Foods (800-780-3663).

PEAR NUTMEG SORBET Add ½ teaspoon ground nutmeg to the blender along with the pears. Proceed with the recipe as directed.

PINEAPPLE SORBET

MAKES ABOUT 1 QUART

FRESH pineapples should smell as sweet as sugar. The inner leaves at the top should pull out easily and there should be very little green. Avoid fruit that has soft spots—a sign that a fruit is damaged or even rotting.

½ cup water

½ cup sugar

1 very ripe small
   pineapple, about
   3 pounds

Juice of 1 lime

Combine the water and sugar in a small saucepan and place over low heat. Stir until the sugar dissolves and the syrup is clear. Remove from heat and allow the syrup to cool to room temperature.

Peel and core the pineapple. Roughly chop the fruit and place in a blender with the cold syrup and lime juice. Blend until very smooth, about 1 minute.

Freeze immediately in your ice cream machine according to the manufacturer's instructions. When finished, the sorbet will be soft but ready to eat. For firmer sorbet, transfer to a freezer-safe container and freeze at least 2 hours.

◂ • ▸

Variations

PINEAPPLE CHERRY SORBET Increase the sugar by 2 tablespoons. Add ½ cup pitted white cherries to the blender along with the pineapple. Proceed with the recipe as directed.

PINEAPPLE CHIPOTLE SORBET Add 2 teaspoons ground chipotle chile powder to the blender along with the fruit. Proceed with the recipe as directed.

PINEAPPLE MANDARIN SORBET Increase the sugar by 3 tablespoons. Add 1 cup drained mandarin orange sections to the blender along with the pineapple. Proceed with the recipe as directed.

POMEGRANATE SORBET

MAKES ABOUT 1 QUART

A LARGE pomegranate can yield almost ½ cup of juice. Simply cut the pomegranate in half and use a citrus juicer to extract the juice—a messy job. Luckily, bottled pomegranate juice is available in many supermarkets and health food stores.

3 cups pomegranate juice,
fresh or bottled

¾ cup sugar

Juice of ½ lime

Place the pomegranate juice in a small saucepan over low heat. When the juice is warm, add the sugar and stir until it is completely dissolved. Remove from the heat and refrigerate until cold or overnight.

Add the lime juice to the chilled mixture and stir well. Freeze in your ice cream machine according to the manufacturer's directions. When finished, the sorbet will be soft but ready to eat. If you like a firmer sorbet, transfer to a freezer-safe container and freeze at least 2 hours.

◄ • ►

Variations

POMEGRANATE CINNAMON SORBET Add two 4-inch cinnamon sticks to the pan with the sugar. Proceed with the recipe as directed, removing the cinnamon sticks before freezing.

POMEGRANATE ORANGE SORBET Substitute 1½ cups orange juice for 1½ cups of the pomegranate juice. Proceed with the recipe as directed, adding 1 teaspoon freshly grated orange zest before freezing.

RUSSIAN POMEGRANATE SORBET Add ½ cup vodka before freezing. Proceed with the recipe as directed.

RASPBERRY SORBET

You can use frozen raspberries instead of fresh berries in this recipe. Just remember to buy whole berries without any sauce or syrup.

1 cup sugar

½ cup water

1 heaping quart fresh
    raspberries, about
    1 pound

Juice of ½ lime

Combine the sugar and water in a small saucepan and place over low heat. Stir until the sugar dissolves and the syrup is clear. Remove from the heat and cool to room temperature.

Place the raspberries in a blender with the cool syrup and lime juice. Blend until completely smooth, about 1 minute. For a smooth sorbet, pour the puree through a strainer to remove the seeds, otherwise freeze immediately in your ice cream machine according to the manufacturer's instructions. When finished, the sorbet will be soft but ready to eat. For firmer sorbet, transfer to a freezer-safe container and freeze at least 2 hours.

◂ • ▸

Variations

RASPBERRY CHAMPAGNE SORBET
Increase the sugar by ¼ cup. Proceed with the recipe as directed, adding 1 cup Champagne to the sorbet mixture before freezing.

RASPBERRY CORDIAL SORBET
Add ½ cup raspberry liqueur before freezing. Proceed with the recipe as directed.

RASPBERRY MARGARITA SORBET
Increase the lime juice to ¼ cup. Add ¼ cup tequila and ¼ cup orange liqueur to the blender along with the lime juice. Proceed with the recipe as directed.

SOUR CHERRY SORBET

FRESH sour cherries may not be readily available in some markets, but jarred, pitted sour cherries are always on the shelf. Use them at will, but be sure to drain the water they're packed in.

¾ cup plus 1 tablespoon
  sugar

⅔ cup water

2 heaping cups pitted sour
  cherries, fresh or canned

Juice of ½ lime

Combine the sugar and water in a small saucepan and place over low heat. Stir until the sugar dissolves and the syrup is clear. Remove from the heat and allow the syrup to cool to room temperature.

Place the cherries in a blender along with the cooled sugar syrup and lime juice. Blend on low until the mixture is smooth, about 30 seconds. Refrigerate until cold or overnight. Stir the chilled mixture, then freeze in your ice cream machine according to the manufacturer's instructions. When finished, the sorbet will be soft but ready to eat. For firmer sorbet, transfer to a freezer-safe container and freeze at least 2 hours.

◂ • ▸

Variations

SOUR CHERRY ALMOND SORBET Add ¼ teaspoon almond extract to the blender along with the cherries. Proceed with the recipe as directed.

SOUR CHERRY WINE SORBET Substitute a hearty red wine (such as cabernet or zinfandel) for the water. Proceed with the recipe as directed.

SWEET CHERRY SORBET Decrease the sugar to ½ cup. Substitute sweet white or red cherries for the sour cherries. Proceed with the recipe as directed.

SWEET CHERRY VANILLA SORBET Decrease the sugar to ½ cup. Substitute sweet white or red cherries for the sour cherries. Add 1 tablespoon vanilla extract to the blender along with the cherries. Proceed with the recipe as directed.

STAR FRUIT SORBET

STAR fruit (sometimes called carambola) is very sweet when yellow and ripe. Don't worry about a little brown around the edges—you can cut that off. The peel is edible, but peeled star fruit makes a smoother sorbet.

3 large ripe star fruits

¼ cup water

6 tablespoons tamarind
 syrup

½ cup superfine sugar

¼ teaspoon salt

Juice of 1 lime

Using a small paring knife, trim any brown edges from the fruit. Gently peel away the thin skin. It may come away easily in some places and be more firmly attached in others. Slice the peeled fruit into 1-inch pieces and use the tip of your knife to remove any seeds. Place the fruit in a blender with the water, tamarind syrup, sugar, salt, and lime juice. Cover and blend for 30 seconds or until the mixture is completely smooth, stopping to scrape down the sides of the blender as necessary.

To avoid any discoloration, freeze immediately in your ice cream machine according to the manufacturer's instructions. The sorbet will be soft but ready to eat. If you prefer your sorbet firmer, simply remove it from your ice cream machine and place it in the freezer for at least 2 hours.

◂ • ▸

Variations

STAR FRUIT ALMOND SORBET Substitute almond syrup for the tamarind syrup. Proceed with the recipe as directed.

STAR FRUIT DAIQUIRI SORBET Add ¼ cup white rum to the blender along with the fruit. Proceed with the recipe as directed.

TEA GRANITA

YOU can make this granita with any tea, including an herbal blend. The amount of sugar can be increased or decreased by as much as ⅓ cup, depending on your taste.

3 cups water

6 tea bags

⅔ cup sugar

Juice of ½ lemon (optional)

Bring the water to a boil, remove from the heat, and add the tea bags. Allow the tea to steep for 5 minutes. Remove the tea bags and add the sugar, stirring until the sugar completely dissolves. Refrigerate until cold. Add the lemon juice.

Freeze in your ice cream machine according to the manufacturer's directions. When finished, the granita will be soft and have the consistency of a sorbet. Transfer to a freezer-safe container and freeze to harden. To serve, scrape the top of the granita with a heavy ice cream spade or scoop, to create shaved ice crystals. Serve in small chilled dishes or hollowed out lemon rinds.

◄ • ►

Variations

APPLE TEA GRANITA Substitute apple herbal tea for the regular tea. Proceed with the recipe as directed. Optional: substitute ⅓ cup maple syrup for ⅓ cup of the sugar.

HONEY TEA GRANITA Substitute ⅓ cup honey for ⅓ cup of the sugar. Proceed with the recipe as directed.

RED ZINGER HONEY GRANITA Substitute Red Zinger tea for the regular tea. Proceed with the recipe as directed.

TOMATO GRANITA

THIS ice makes a lovely first course in lieu of a chilled soup. To serve, cut a lemon in half lengthwise, then scoop out the inside creating a shell. Fill with sorbet and set in a bed of rock salt to keep it from falling over. Garnish with fresh basil leaves.

2 pounds ripe tomatoes

2 tablespoons honey

1 tablespoon sugar

1/4 teaspoon salt

To peel the tomatoes, drop them in boiling water for 30 seconds, then transfer them to a bowl of ice water. The skins should slip right off. Cut the peeled tomatoes into quarters and scoop out the seeds with your fingers. Place the tomatoes in a food processor with the honey, sugar, and salt. Process until the mixture is completely smooth.

Freeze in your ice cream machine according to the manufacturer's directions. When finished, the granita will be soft and have the consistency of a sorbet. Transfer to a freezer-safe container and freeze to harden. To serve, scrape the top of the granita with a heavy ice cream spade or scoop, to create shaved ice crystals. Serve in small chilled dishes.

Alternately, pour the tomato mixture into ice cube trays, filling only half way, and freeze until firm. Before serving, process the tomato ice cubes in a food processor until chopped and slushy. Serve immediately.

‹ • ›

Variations

CURRIED TOMATO GRANITA
Add 2 teaspoons curry powder to the food processor along with the tomatoes. Proceed with the recipe as directed.

TEXAS TOMATO GRANITA
Add 1 tablespoon chopped pickled jalapeño to the food processor along with the tomatoes. Proceed with the recipe as directed.

TOMATO ORANGE GRANITA
Add 2 tablespoons orange juice concentrate to the food processor along with the tomatoes. Proceed with the recipe as directed.

WATERMELON SORBET

IF you can find them, seedless watermelons make this a very simple dessert to prepare.

1 small watermelon, about
5 pounds

½ cup light corn syrup

½ cup sugar

Juice of 2 limes, about
3 tablespoons

2 tablespoons grenadine

Cut the rind off the melon and discard. Working over a large bowl, use your hands to break up the fruit and get rid of the seeds. Place half the fruit and accumulated juice into a blender with the corn syrup. Blend until the mixture is liquefied. Pour through a strainer into a pitcher or a clean bowl. Repeat with the remaining fruit and sugar. Add the lime juice and grenadine to the watermelon puree. Cover and refrigerate until cold or overnight. This may be made up to 3 days in advance.

Freeze in your ice cream machine according to the manufacturer's directions. When finished, the sorbet will be soft but ready to eat. If you like a firmer sorbet, transfer to a freezer-safe container and freeze at least 2 hours.

‹ • ›

Variations

"HOT" WATERMELON SORBET Add 1 teaspoon (or more to taste) Tabasco sauce to the blender along with the fruit. Proceed with the recipe as directed.

WATERMELON APRICOT SORBET Substitute 1 cup apricot nectar for 1 cup of the pureed watermelon. Proceed with the recipe as directed.

WATERMELON PINEAPPLE SORBET Substitute 1 cup drained canned crushed pineapple for 1 cup of the broken up watermelon chunks. Proceed with the recipe as directed.

Ice Cream Toppings

THESE TOPPINGS ARE PERFECT FOR SUNDAES, PARFAITS, BANANA SPLITS, OR SIMPLY SPOONING AND POURING OVER ANY FLAVOR OF ICE CREAM.

APPLE SPICE TOPPING

MAKES ABOUT 2 CUPS

CERTAIN types of apples hold their shape when cooked: Rome, Granny Smith, Braeburn, and McIntosh. Look for these apples when making this topping.

1 teaspoon cornstarch

Juice of ½ lemon

2 tablespoons unsalted butter

3 medium apples, peeled (about 1¼ pounds)

2 tablespoons brandy or apple juice

⅓ cup granulated sugar

¼ cup light brown sugar

½ teaspoon ground cinnamon

⅛ teaspoon ground nutmeg

⅛ teaspoon ground cloves

1 teaspoon vanilla extract

In a small bowl, dissolve the cornstarch in the lemon juice and set aside.

Melt the butter in a large heavy sauté pan. Slice the apples into 1⁄2-inch pieces and cook, stirring, in the hot butter until the fruit begins to soften, 5 to 10 minutes. Add the brandy, being very careful to keep the pan away from you as the brandy may flame. Add the granulated sugar, brown sugar, cinnamon, nutmeg, and cloves. Cook until the sugars dissolve and begin to caramelize, about 3 minutes. Add the lemon juice–cornstarch mixture. As soon as the sauce thickens, remove from the heat. Stir in the vanilla. Serve warm or at room temperature.

Variations

APPLE JACK TOPPING Substitute calvados or apple brandy for the brandy. Proceed with the recipe as directed.

APPLE NUT TOPPING Add 1 cup chopped toasted pecans (see page xvi) along with the lemon juice–cornstarch mixture. Proceed with the recipe as directed.

DARK CARAMEL APPLE TOPPING Substitute ½ cup dark brown sugar for the granulated sugar and light brown sugar. Add 2 teaspoons molasses along with the brown sugar. Proceed with the recipe as directed.

BANANA TOPPING

THIS topping is best served warm. Do not prepare it more than two hours in advance or the bananas may turn the sauce a dark brown.

¼ cup (½ stick) unsalted
  butter
4 small bananas, about
  1 pound
½ cup sugar
¼ teaspoon ground
  cinnamon
⅛ teaspoon ground nutmeg
2 tablespoons banana
  liqueur or syrup (optional)
1 teaspoon vanilla extract

Melt the butter in a large, heavy sauté pan. Peel and slice the bananas into ½-inch pieces. Cook the bananas in the hot butter, stirring, until the fruit begins to soften, about 2 minutes. Add the sugar, cinnamon, and nutmeg. Cook until the sugar dissolves and begins to caramelize, about 2 minutes. Add the banana liqueur and vanilla. Serve warm or at room temperature.

Variations

BANANA ALMOND TOPPING Substitute amaretto liqueur or almond syrup for the banana liqueur. Proceed with the recipe as directed, adding ¼ cup sliced toasted almonds (see page xvi) at the last moment before serving.

BANANA MARSHMALLOW TOPPING Add ½ cup mini-marshmallows along with the vanilla, and stir until the marshmallows melt completely. Serve immediately.

BANANA RUM RAISIN TOPPING Pour 2 tablespoons dark rum over ¼ cup raisins and set aside for 1 hour before preparing the sauce. Omit the banana liqueur. Add the raisins and rum along with the vanilla. Heat through and serve immediately.

BANANA WALNUT TOPPING Add ½ cup chopped walnuts at the last moment before serving.

BUTTERSCOTCH SAUCE

MELTING butterscotch chips is the easiest way to make butterscotch sauce with a rich butterscotch taste. Adding cream, butter, and brown sugar enhances the creamy texture.

¾ cup heavy cream

2 tablespoons unsalted
   butter

2 tablespoons light brown
   sugar

one 11-ounce bag
   butterscotch chips

Combine the cream, butter, and brown sugar in a small saucepan. Place over low heat and stir until the sugar dissolves, the butter melts, and the cream comes to a simmer. Pour the hot cream over the butterscotch chips in a large metal bowl. Stir until the chips are melted and the sauce is smooth. Serve warm or at room temperature.

‹ • • ›

Variations

BUTTERSCOTCH BANANA CHIP TOPPING Add ½ cup finely chopped dried banana chips after the butterscotch chips have melted. Proceed with the recipe as directed.

BUTTERSCOTCH CHOCOLATE TOPPING Substitute chocolate chips for ½ of the butterscotch chips. Proceed with the recipe as directed.

BUTTERSCOTCH NUT TOPPING Add ½ cup chopped toasted hazelnuts (see page xvi) after the chips have melted. Proceed with the recipe as directed.

BUTTERSCOTCH RUM TOPPING Add 2 tablespoons dark rum after the chips have melted. Proceed with the recipe as directed.

CARAMEL SAUCE

WORKING with caramel can be dangerous—it can reach temperatures over 350°F. Warming the cream helps reduce the splattering and the possibility of a burn.

1 cup heavy cream, warmed

1 cup sugar

½ cup water

1 teaspoon vanilla extract

Place the cream in a small saucepan set over low heat. Cover and keep the cream warm while you make the caramel.

Combine the sugar and water in a large, heavy saucepan and place over medium heat. Stir until the sugar dissolves and the syrup is clear. As the syrup boils, use a wet pastry brush to wash down any sugar crystals that form on the sides of the pan. Continue to cook without stirring until the syrup turns golden brown. Immediately remove from the heat and slowly add the warm cream, stirring constantly. The caramel will spit and rise up, so do this carefully. The sugar may also form a clump on the bottom of the pan. Return the pan to a low heat and stir until the caramel dissolves into the cream completely. Let simmer for 2 minutes. Remove from the heat and stir in the vanilla. Serve warm or at room temperature.

◄ • ►

Variations

CARAMEL NUT TOPPING Add ½ cup chopped toasted nuts (see page xvi) along with the vanilla. Nuts of choice include peanuts, walnuts, almonds, pecans, hazelnuts, brazil nuts, macadamia nuts, or cashews.

CARAMEL RAISIN TOPPING Add ½ cup plump golden raisins long with the vanilla.

CHOCOLATE SAUCE

THE perfect foil for nearly any flavor ice cream . . . or dessert, for that matter.

¼ cup unsalted butter

2 ounces unsweetened
chocolate

¾ cup sugar

2 tablespoons unsweetened
cocoa powder

½ cup heavy cream

2 teaspoons vanilla extract

Melt the butter and chocolate together in a double boiler or in a large metal bowl set over a pan of simmering water. Combine the sugar and cocoa in another bowl. Stir the heavy cream into the sugar and cocoa and mix until a thick paste forms. Stir the chocolate paste into the melted chocolate and butter. Cook the mixture over simmering water for 5 minutes, stirring constantly. Whisk in the vanilla. Serve warm or room temperature.

◄ • ►

Variations

CHOCOLATE ESPRESSO SAUCE Add 2 teaspoons instant espresso powder along with the cocoa. Proceed with the recipe as directed.

CHOCOLATE MARSHMALLOW SAUCE Add ½ cup mini-marshmallows to the finished sauce. Stir until the marshmallows melt completely.

CHOCOLATE WHISKEY SAUCE Add ¼ cup whiskey along with the vanilla. Heat through.

MEXICAN CHOCOLATE SAUCE Add ½ teaspoon ground cinnamon along with the cocoa. Proceed with the recipe as directed. Add ¼ teaspoon almond extract and ½ cup chopped toasted almonds (see page xvi) along with the vanilla.

TEXAS CHOCOLATE SAUCE Add ½ teaspoon crushed red pepper flakes (or more to taste) along with the cocoa powder.

CHOCOLATE SYRUP

THIS syrup is easy to make and virtually fat free. It's great on ice cream or in milk, and perfect for chocolate sodas or egg creams.

1½ cups sugar

½ cup light corn syrup

1½ cups water

1 cup unsweetened cocoa
    powder

1 tablespoon vanilla extract

Combine the sugar, corn syrup, and water in a large, heavy saucepan and place over medium heat. Stir until the sugar dissolves and the syrup is clear. Boil for 5 minutes without stirring. Reduce the heat to low and slowly whisk in the cocoa. Bring back to a simmer and cook 1 minute, stirring constantly. Remove from the heat and cool to room temperature. Stir in vanilla.

Variations

CHOCOLATE ALMOND SYRUP Add ¼ teaspoon almond extract along with the vanilla.

CHOCOLATE MINT SYRUP Substitute ½ teaspoon peppermint extract for the vanilla extract.

CHOCOLATE ORANGE SYRUP Add ¼ teaspoon orange oil (available at candy and baking supply stores or by calling Central Market in Austin, Texas, at 800-360-2552) along with the vanilla.

CHOCOLATE RUM SYRUP Add 2 tablespoons dark rum along with the vanilla.

HONEY SAUCE

MAKES 1 ½ CUPS

USE a light, fragrant honey such as orange blossom or wildflower, and do not refrigerate this sauce because it may crystallize.

¼ cup sugar

2 tablespoons light corn syrup

2 tablespoons water

1 cup mild honey

Combine the sugar, corn syrup, and water in a medium saucepan. Stir over low heat until the sugar dissolves completely. Raise the heat to medium, bring to a boil, and boil for 2 minutes. Remove from the heat and stir in the honey. Serve warm or at room temperature.

◄ • ►

Variations

HONEY CORDIAL SAUCE Add ½ cup Bärenjäger, a honey-based liqueur, along with the honey.

HONEY ROSEMARY SAUCE Add 3 fresh rosemary sprigs to the pan along with the sugar. When finished, allow the rosemary to remain in the sauce, as the flavor will get stronger. But do not serve the rosemary with the sauce.

HOT FUDGE SAUCE

THIS topping is perhaps the classic of all classics.

4 ounces bittersweet or
semisweet chocolate,
chopped

2 ounces unsweetened
chocolate, chopped

3 tablespoons unsalted
butter

⅓ cup heavy cream

⅓ cup sugar

⅓ cup light corn syrup

1 teaspoon vanilla extract

Melt the bittersweet and unsweetened chocolates with the butter in a double boiler, or in a large metal bowl set over a pot of simmering water.

Meanwhile, warm the cream in a medium saucepan over low heat. Add the sugar and corn syrup to the cream and stir until the sugar dissolves completely. Add the warm sweetened cream to the melted chocolate. Continue to heat the mixture over simmering water for 10 minutes, stirring constantly. Add the vanilla. Serve hot.

Variations

CHERRY FUDGE SAUCE Pour 2 tablespoons cherry brandy over ¼ cup dried cherries and set aside for 1 hour before preparing the sauce. Add the cherries and liqueur along with the vanilla.

MARSHMALLOW FUDGE MELTDOWN Add 1 cup mini-marshmallows and ½ cup chopped toasted hazelnuts (see page xvi) along with the vanilla. Stir until the marshmallows melt completely.

SOUTHERN FUDGE SAUCE Add ½ cup chopped toasted pecans (see page xvi) along with the vanilla.

TROPICAL FUDGE SAUCE Add ½ cup toasted sweetened coconut (see page xvi) along with the vanilla. Optional: add 2 tablespoons coconut-flavored rum.

LEMON SAUCE

FOR a truly unique flavor combination, try this sauce warm over Chocolate Truffle Ice Cream (page 44) or Raspberry Sorbet (page 178).

1 tablespoon plus
  1 teaspoon cornstarch
1 cup sugar
1 cup water
⅔ cup fresh lemon juice
1 teaspoon lemon extract
5 tablespoons unsalted
  butter, at room
  temperature
2 drops yellow food
  coloring (optional)

Combine all of the ingredients in the top of a double boiler, or in a metal mixing bowl set over a pan of simmering water. Whisk constantly until the sauce is thickened, smooth, and translucent, about 15 minutes. Serve warm or at room temperature.

‹ • • ›

Variations

LEMON COCONUT SAUCE Add ¼ cup toasted sweetened coconut (see page xvi) along with the vanilla. Optional: add 2 tablespoons coconut-flavored rum.

LEMON HONEY SAUCE Substitute ½ cup honey for ½ cup of the sugar.

LEMON LICORICE SAUCE Add 2 tablespoons chopped black licorice candy to the finished sauce.

MARSHMALLOW SAUCE

MAKES ABOUT 3 CUPS

THIS sauce is delicious, hot or cold. It reheats well in the microwave or in a small bowl set over a pan of simmering water.

2 large egg whites

1 cup sugar

½ cup water

16 regular marshmallows

½ teaspoon vanilla extract

In a mixing bowl, beat the egg whites until soft peaks form. Set aside.

Combine the sugar and water in a medium saucepan and place over medium heat. Stir until the sugar dissolves, then let the mixture boil for 3 minutes. Reduce the heat to low, add the marshmallows, and stir until they are completely melted and the mixture is smooth. Remove from heat and slowly beat the hot marshmallow mixture into the egg whites. Continue to beat for 2 minutes. Beat in the vanilla extract. Serve hot or cold.

‹ • ›

Variations

MARSHMALLOW CARAMEL SAUCE Add 8 small caramel candies along with the marshmallows. Stir until the candies are melted completely.

MARSHMALLOW COCONUT SAUCE Add ¼ cup shredded sweetened coconut along with the vanilla. Optional: add 2 tablespoons coconut-flavored rum.

MARSHMALLOW MINT SAUCE Substitute ½ teaspoon peppermint extract for the vanilla extract.

MARSHMALLOW NUT SAUCE Add ½ cup chopped toasted almonds, hazelnuts, or pecans (see page xvi) to the finished sauce.

PEACH TOPPING

THIS topping is somewhere between a sauce and pie filling. You can use fresh or frozen peaches, but frozen do come already peeled.

1½ pounds peaches,
   peeled and thinly sliced
1 cup sugar
½ cup orange juice
Juice of ½ lemon

Place all of the ingredients in a large, heavy saucepan. Set over medium heat and stir until the sugar is dissolved and the mixture comes to a simmer. Cook, stirring frequently, for 10 minutes. Serve warm or cold.

◂ • ▸

Variations

PEACH ALMOND TOPPING Add ¼ teaspoon almond extract along with the peaches. Optional: add ¼ cup chopped, toasted almonds (see page xvi) when the sauce is finished.

PEACHCOT TOPPING Substitute ¾ pound fresh apricots for ¾ pound of the peaches. Proceed with the recipe as directed.

SPICED PEACH TOPPING Add ¼ teaspoon ground cinnamon and ⅛ teaspoon ground nutmeg to the pan along with the peaches.

PEANUT BUTTER SAUCE

THIS sauce is a paradox: the addition of marshmallows helps make it light and fluffy while evaporated milk keeps it rich and creamy—all at the same time.

¾ cup evaporated milk, or
more as needed

⅔ cup light corn syrup

4 regular marshmallows

⅔ cup smooth peanut
butter

1 teaspoon vanilla extract

Combine the evaporated milk, corn syrup, and marshmallows in a large, heavy saucepan. Place over medium heat and stir constantly until the marshmallows melt completely and the sauce simmers for 1 minute. Remove from the heat and whisk in the peanut butter and vanilla. If the sauce thickens too much as it cools, thin it with additional evaporated milk, 1 tablespoon at a time until the desired consistency is reached. Serve warm or at room temperature.

‹ • ›

Variations

PEANUT BUTTER BANANA SAUCE Add 2 bananas, thinly sliced, immediately before serving.

PEANUT BUTTER BERRY SAUCE Add ¼ cup fresh or frozen blueberries, sliced strawberries, raspberries, or blackberries immediately before serving.

PEANUTS AND MORE PEANUT SAUCE Add ½ cup chopped dry-roasted peanuts to the finished sauce.

PINEAPPLE TOPPING

CANNED pineapple chunks are great for this recipe, but you can substitute crushed pineapple if you prefer a less chunky topping.

one 20-ounce can
pineapple chunks in
unsweetened juice
Juice of ½ lemon
1 cup sugar

Drain the pineapple, reserving the juice. Combine the pineapple juice and lemon juice with the sugar in a large heavy saucepan. Place over medium heat and stir until the sugar dissolves and the mixture comes to a simmer. Cook the syrup for 10 minutes. Add the pineapple and bring the syrup back to a simmer. Cook for an additional 10 minutes or until the syrup has reduced and thickened slightly. Serve warm or cold.

Variations

HAWAIIAN TOPPING Add ¼ cup gold rum and ¼ cup chopped macadamia nuts to the pan along with the pineapple. Proceed with the recipe as directed.

PINEAPPLE COCONUT TOPPING Add ¼ cup shredded sweetened coconut along with the pineapple. Proceed with the recipe as directed. Optional: add 2 tablespoons coconut-flavored rum.

ZESTY PINEAPPLE SAUCE Add 1 seeded and chopped fresh jalapeño to the pan along with the pineapple. Proceed with the recipe as directed.

STRAWBERRY TOPPING

MAKES 1½ CUPS

BE careful not to overcook this topping; otherwise, you'll want to serve it on toast instead of ice cream.

1½ quarts strawberries

1 cup sugar

Juice of 1 lime

Slice the berries in half and place them in a large, heavy saucepan with the sugar and lime juice. Toss well and let the berries sit for 2 hours to release their juice. Place the pot over medium heat and stir until the sugar is completely dissolved and the mixture comes to a simmer. Cook, stirring frequently, for 10 minutes. Serve cold or at room temperature.

Variations

STRAWBERRY ALMOND TOPPING Add ¼ teaspoon almond extract and ¼ cup chopped toasted almonds (see page xvi) to the pan along with the strawberries.

STRAWBERRY DAIQUIRI TOPPING Add 2 tablespoons white rum to the finished sauce.

STRAWBERRY RHUBARB TOPPING Slice rhubarb into ½-inch pieces and steam for 10 minutes or until tender. Increase the sugar by ⅓ cup and proceed with the recipe as directed, adding the rhubarb to the pan just before bringing the berries to a simmer.

TROPICAL FRUIT TOPPING

THIS topping requires absolutely no cooking.

1 ripe mango, peeled,
   pitted, and finely
   chopped

1 ripe papaya, peeled,
   seeded, and finely
   chopped

2 tablespoons fresh lime
   juice

2 tablespoons passion fruit
   concentrate or syrup

2 tablespoons sugar

¼ cup shredded sweetened
   coconut

Combine all of the ingredients in a large bowl and mix well. Cover and refrigerate at least 4 hours to allow the flavors to blend. Serve cold.

◂ • ▸

Variations

TROPICAL DAIQUIRI TOPPING Add 3 tablespoons gold rum along with the fruit.

TROPICAL MARTINI TOPPING Add 3 tablespoons dry vermouth or other sweet white wine along with the fruit.

TROPICAL THAI TOPPING Add ½ teaspoon Thai yellow curry paste along with the fruit.

WET WALNUT TOPPING

I F there is a holy trinity of toppings for sundaes and banana splits, it would most likely include hot fudge, strawberry, and wet nuts. This version of wet walnuts is sweet, sticky, and full of rich walnut flavor.

1 cup sugar

1 cup light corn syrup

1 cup water

2 cups roughly chopped walnuts

Combine the sugar, corn syrup, and water in a large, heavy saucepan and place over medium heat. Stir until the sugar dissolves and the syrup is clear. Boil for 2 minutes without stirring. Add the walnuts, bring back to a boil, and cook for 2 minutes, stirring constantly. Remove from the heat and allow to cool. Serve and store at room temperature. Stir well before serving.

Variations

FALL WALNUT TOPPING Add ¼ cup raisins and ¼ cup chopped dried figs along with the nuts. Proceed with the recipe as indicated.

WALNUT WHISKEY TOPPING Add ¼ cup whiskey to the finished topping.

WHITE CHOCOLATE SAUCE

USE premium white chocolate for this sauce. Avoid white baking chips, which are not really chocolate at all.

½ cup heavy cream

1 tablespoon unsalted
   butter

½ pound white chocolate,
   chopped

1 teaspoon vanilla extract

2 tablespoons white crème
   de cacao (optional)

Combine the cream and butter in a small saucepan. Place over low heat until the butter melts and the cream comes to a simmer. Pour the hot cream over the chocolate in a bowl, stirring until the chocolate is completely melted and the mixture is smooth and creamy. Stir in the vanilla and crème de cacao. Serve warm or at room temperature.

◂ • ▸

Variations

WHITE CHOCOLATE ALMOND SAUCE Substitute amaretto liqueur for the crème de cacao. Add ½ cup chopped toasted almonds (see page xvi) to the finished sauce.

WHITE CHOCOLATE CINNAMON SAUCE Add ½ teaspoon ground cinnamon to the pan along with the cream and butter.

WHITE CHOCOLATE HAZELNUT SAUCE Substitute hazelnut liqueur for the crème de cacao. Add ½ cup chopped toasted hazelnuts (see page xvi) to the finished sauce.

WHITE CHOCOLATE RUM SAUCE Add 3 tablespoons gold rum or coconut-flavored rum to the finished sauce.

Ice Cream Drinks—Sodas, Shakes, and Malts

BANANA THICK SHAKE

MAKES TWO 16-OUNCE DRINKS

To enhance the flavor, use banana liqueur or banana-flavored syrup, available in many gourmet stores, such as Central Market (800-360-2552).

2 small bananas

1½ cups ice cubes

3 scoops vanilla ice cream, softened

½ cup pineapple juice or apple juice

¼ cup banana liqueur or syrup

1 tablespoon honey

Combine all of the ingredients in a blender. Blend until the mixture is smooth, about 30 seconds. If necessary, pulse the blender on and off until the mixture blends easily.

Variations

BANANA COCONUT SHAKE Substitute ¼ cup sweetened cream of coconut for banana liqueur. Proceed with the recipe as directed.

BANANA MALT Add 2 tablespoons malted milk powder. Substitute whole milk for fruit juice. Proceed with the recipe as directed.

CHOCOLATE-COVERED BANANA Substitute chocolate ice cream for vanilla ice cream. Substitute chocolate syrup for fruit juice. Proceed with the recipe as directed.

CREAMY BANANA COCKTAIL Substitute gold or spiced rum for fruit juice. Proceed with the recipe as directed.

SPICED BANANA SHAKE Add ¼ teaspoon ground cinnamon, ⅛ teaspoon ground nutmeg, and ½ teaspoon vanilla extract to the blender along with the banana. Proceed with the recipe as directed.

BLACK AND WHITE ICE CREAM SODA

START with premium ice cream so you'll have a premium ice cream soda.

2 tablespoons chocolate
  syrup
8 to 12 ounces plain
  unsweetened soda water
2 scoops premium vanilla
  ice cream

Place the chocolate syrup in the bottom of a chilled 16-ounce glass. Add 4 ounces of soda water and stir until well blended. Add 1 scoop of ice cream. Fill the glass with the remaining soda water. Top with the remaining scoop of ice cream, pressing it firmly on the rim of the glass to prevent it from falling in.

‹ • • ›

Variations

BLACK ON BLACK ICE CREAM SODA Substitute rich dark chocolate ice cream for vanilla ice cream.

CHOCOLATE FLOAT Substitute cola for soda water.

MEXICAN CHOCOLATE SODA Add ⅛ teaspoon ground cinnamon and 2 drops almond extract along with the chocolate syrup.

BLACK COW ICE CREAM SODA

MAKES ONE 16-OUNCE DRINK

FOR a frosted treat, chill the glass in your freezer at least five minutes before making this drink.

1½ tablespoons chocolate syrup

8 to 12 ounces root beer

2 scoops premium vanilla ice cream

Place the chocolate syrup in the bottom of a chilled 16-ounce glass. Add 4 ounces of the root beer and stir until well blended. Add one scoop of ice cream. Fill the glass with the remaining root beer. Top with the remaining scoop of ice cream, pressing it firmly onto the rim of the glass to prevent it from falling in.

◂ • • ▸

Variations

BROWN COW ICE CREAM SODA Substitute cola for root beer.

OLD-FASHIONED ROOT BEER FLOAT Omit the chocolate syrup.

ROOT BEER CHERRY FLOAT Substitute cherry syrup for chocolate.

ROOT BEER ICE CREAM COCKTAIL Add 2 tablespoons dark rum along with the chocolate syrup.

BRANDY ALEXANDER FREEZE

Use any good but inexpensive brandy for this chilly libation.

1½ cups ice cubes

2 tablespoons brandy

2 tablespoons white or
dark crème de cacao

1 tablespoon chocolate
syrup

2 scoops premium vanilla
ice cream, softened

Combine all of the ingredients in a blender. Blend until the mixture is smooth, about 30 seconds. If necessary, pulse the blender on and off until the mixture blends easily.

Variations

CHOCOLATE BANANA BANSHEE Add ½ banana and 2 tablespoons crème de banana liqueur before blending. Makes two 8-ounce cocktails.

RASPBERRY CHOCOLATE BUZZ Add ½ cup raspberries and 2 tablespoons raspberry liqueur before blending. Makes two 8-ounce cocktails.

STRAWBERRY BRANDY ALEXANDER Add ¼ cup strawberry jam or strawberry topping (see page 200) before blending.

CHERRY CHEESECAKE THICK SHAKE

MAKES TWO 12-OUNCE DRINKS

RICH, sweet, and creamy—this drink really does taste like cherry cheesecake à la mode!

1 cup pitted sweet cherries,
fresh or canned

3 heaping tablespoons
powdered no-bake
cheesecake mix

1½ cups ice cubes

2 scoops vanilla ice cream,
regular or low-fat

Place the cherries in the freezer until semifrozen, about 2 hours. Combine the cherries and the remaining ingredients in a blender. Blend until smooth, about 30 seconds. If necessary, pulse the blender on and off until the mixture blends easily and reaches a smooth consistency.

Variations

BLUEBERRY CHEESECAKE SHAKE Substitute 1 cup blueberries for the cherries.

CHOCOLATE CHEESECAKE SHAKE Substitute ¼ cup chocolate syrup and 4 crumbled chocolate cookies for the cherries.

MALTED CHEESECAKE SHAKE Substitute 1 tablespoon malted milk powder, ½ cup whole milk, and ½ teaspoon vanilla extract for the cherries.

PINEAPPLE CHEESECAKE SHAKE Substitute 1 cup pineapple chunks for the cherries.

STRAWBERRY CHEESECAKE SHAKE Substitute 1 cup sliced strawberries for the cherries.

CHOCOLATE MALT

Low-fat ice cream and skim milk will give you a low-fat variation with just as much flavor.

3 scoops premium
  chocolate ice cream
¼ cup chocolate syrup
¾ cup milk
1½ cups ice cubes
3 heaping tablespoons
  malted milk powder

Combine all of the ingredients in a blender. Blend until smooth, about 30 seconds. If necessary, pulse the blender on and off until the mixture blends easily and reaches a smooth consistency.

◄ • ►

Variations

CHOCOLATE CHERRY MALT Add ¼ cup pitted fresh cherries before blending.

CHOCOLATE PEANUT BUTTER MALT Add 2 tablespoons peanut butter and 1 peanut butter cup candy bar before blending.

MEXICAN CHOCOLATE MALT Add ¼ teaspoon ground cinnamon and 2 tablespoons chopped toasted almonds (see page xvi) before blending.

COFFEE THICK SHAKE

FOR extra coffee flavor, fill ice cube trays half way with freshly brewed coffee. Then use the coffee ice cubes instead of regular ice.

1 tablespoon instant coffee
    powder

2 tablespoons water

1½ cups ice cubes

¼ cup coffee syrup

3 scoops coffee ice cream,
    softened

½ cup milk

Dissolve the instant coffee in the water. Add this to a blender along with the remaining ingredients. Blend until the mixture is smooth. If necessary, pulse the blender on and off until the mixture blends easily.

Variations

CHOCOLATE RASPBERRY COFFEE SHAKE Add ½ cup fresh raspberries and ¼ cup chocolate syrup before blending.

COFFEE ALMOND SHAKE Add ¼ teaspoon almond extract before blending.

COFFEE MALT Add 2 tablespoons malted milk powder before blending.

HAZELNUT COFFEE THICK SHAKE Substitute hazelnut syrup for coffee syrup.

ICED COFFEE COCKTAIL Substitute coffee liqueur for coffee syrup, and add ¼ cup coffee-flavored vodka and ½ cup extra ice cubes before blending. Makes two 16-ounce drinks.

MOCHA THICK SHAKE Substitute chocolate syrup for coffee syrup. If a stronger chocolate flavor is desired, use chocolate ice cream instead of coffee ice cream.

GRASSHOPPER MIST

MAKES TWO 8-OUNCE DRINKS

CHOCOLATE and mint liqueurs give this cocktail its traditional color and flavor. For more intense flavor, use mint chip ice cream instead of vanilla.

1 cup ice cubes

2 scoops vanilla or mint chip ice cream, softened

2 tablespoons vodka

3 tablespoons white crème de cacao

1 tablespoon green crème de menthe

1 chocolate-covered peppermint candy (1.5 ounces), crumbled

Place all of the ingredients in a blender. Blend until the mixture is smooth, about 30 seconds. If necessary, pulse the blender on and off until the mixture blends easily.

◄ • ►

Variation

ZERO-PROOF MINT SHAKE Omit the vodka. Substitute chocolate syrup for crème de cacao and ¼ teaspoon peppermint extract for crème de menthe.

LEMON DROP COCKTAIL

THIS slushy cocktail can be made with plain vodka, lemon vodka, or an Italian lemon-flavored liqueur called Lemoncello.

2 scoops lemon sorbet
4 ice cubes
2 tablespoons vodka

Combine all of the ingredients in a blender. Pulse the blender on and off until the mixture blends easily. Blend on high for 30 seconds or until smooth.

Variations

CHOCOLATE EXPLOSION Substitute chocolate sorbet for lemon sorbet. If desired, add ½ tablespoon chocolate liqueur before blending.

PEACH BOMB Substitute peach sorbet for lemon sorbet. If desired, add ½ tablespoon peach schnapps before blending.

PEAR BLAST Substitute pear sorbet for lemon sorbet. If desired, add ½ tablespoon pear liqueur before blending.

RASPBERRY BLAST Substitute raspberry sorbet for lemon sorbet. If desired, add ½ tablespoon raspberry liqueur before blending.

LEMON-LIME RICKEY

U SE 7-Up, Sprite, or any other lemon-lime-flavored soda for this drink.

12 ounces lemon-lime soda, chilled
2 tablespoons lime-flavored syrup
2 scoops lemon sorbet

Fill a chilled 16-ounce glass three-quarters full with the lemon-lime soda. Carefully pour the lime syrup down the side of the glass so that it sinks to the bottom of the soda without mixing in. Top with 1 scoop of lemon sorbet. Press the second scoop of sorbet onto the rim of the glass to prevent it from falling in.

◄ • ►

Variations

CHERRY LEMON-LIME RICKEY Substitute sweet cherry soda for lemon-lime soda.

LEMON-LIME RICKEY COCKTAIL Add 3 tablespoons white rum to the glass before adding soda.

MANDARIN VANILLA SHAKE

THIS old-time favorite makes a great treat for kids—and adults, with the addition of a little orange liqueur and rum.

1½ cups canned mandarin
  orange segments,
  drained
1½ cups ice cubes
3 scoops vanilla ice cream
2 tablespoons orange juice
  concentrate, defrosted

Combine all of the ingredients in a blender. Blend until smooth, about 30 seconds. If necessary, pulse the blender on and off until the mixture blends easily.

‹ • • ›

Variations

CHOCOLATE ORANGE SHAKE Substitute chocolate ice cream for vanilla ice cream. Add ¼ teaspoon ground cinnamon before blending.

MANDARIN CHOCOLATE SHAKE Substitute ¼ cup chocolate syrup for orange juice concentrate.

MANDARIN COCKTAIL Add ¼ cup orange liqueur, ¼ cup gold rum, and ½ cup additional ice cubes before blending. Makes two 16-ounce drinks.

SPICED ORANGE SHAKE Add ¼ teaspoon almond extract, ¼ teaspoon ground cinnamon, and a pinch of ground cloves before blending.

MANGO FREEZE

MAKES TWO 12-OUNCE DRINKS

F your mangoes are hard, place them in a paper bag and store at room temperature for a few days, or until they soften and smell sweet.

1 large ripe mango

1½ cups ice cubes

¾ cup mango nectar or
  peach nectar

3 scoops vanilla ice cream,
  softened

1 tablespoon honey

Peel the mango and cut away as much meat from the large hard pit as possible. Place the mango pieces into a blender with the remaining ingredients. Blend until the mixture is smooth, about 30 seconds. If necessary, pulse the blender on and off and add additional nectar 1 tablespoon at a time, until the mixture blends easily.

‹ • ›

Variations

MANGO APRICOT FREEZE Substitute apricot nectar for mango nectar.

MANGO PASSION FRUIT FREEZE Substitute ¼ cup passion fruit concentrate and ½ cup orange juice for mango nectar.

MANGO PEACH COCKTAIL Substitute peach sorbet for ice cream. Substitute ¼ cup gold or spiced rum, ⅓ cup peach schnapps, and 2 tablespoons bottled sweetened lime juice for mango nectar.

MANGO PEACH FREEZE Substitute peach ice cream for vanilla ice cream. Use grenadine instead of honey.

PEACH MELBA COCKTAIL

THIS classic combination of peaches and raspberries makes a great cocktail using sorbet, and a terrific shake using ice cream.

1 large peach, pitted

1½ cups ice cubes

1 cup raspberries

½ cup gold rum

2 scoops peach sorbet

2 tablespoons raspberry liqueur

¼ teaspoon vanilla extract

Cut the peach into eighths and place in a blender with the remaining ingredients. Pulse the blender on and off until the mixture blends easily. Blend on high for 30 seconds or until smooth.

PEACH MELBA SHAKE

MAKES TWO 12-OUNCE DRINKS

1 large peach, pitted

1½ cups ice cubes

1 cup raspberries

½ cup peach nectar

2 scoops vanilla ice cream

2 tablespoons vanilla syrup

Cut the peach into small pieces and place in a blender along with the remaining ingredients. Blend until the mixture is smooth, about 30 seconds. If necessary, pulse the blender on and off until the mixture blends easily.

◂ • ▸

Variation

SPICY PEACH BLAST (COCKTAIL OR SHAKE) Add ¼ teaspoon ground cinnamon, ⅛ teaspoon ground nutmeg, and ⅛ teaspoon ground mace to either peach drink before blending.

STRAWBERRY MALT

FRESH or frozen strawberries will work here. In fact, if you use fresh berries, you should partially freeze them before blending. If you use frozen berries, defrost them partially before blending.

12 large strawberries, partially frozen

2 scoops strawberries ice cream

3 heaping tablespoons malted milk powder

1 cup milk

2 tablespoons strawberry topping or strawberry preserves

Place all of the ingredients in a blender. Pulse the blender on and off until the mixture blends easily. Blend on high for 30 seconds or until smooth.

◀ • ▶

Variations

STRAWBERRY COCONUT MALT Substitute unsweetened coconut milk for the dairy milk.

VERY STRAWBERRY MALT If you prefer a plain strawberry shake, simply omit the malted milk powder.

TROPICAL THICK SHAKE

ALMOST any combination of tropical fruits and juices will work. The trick is using both sweet and tart fruit flavors.

1 cup ice cubes

2 kiwi, peeled and
    quartered

½ banana, peeled and
    sliced

½ cup guava nectar

½ cup passion fruit juice

3 scoops vanilla ice cream

Place all of the ingredients in a blender. Blend until smooth, about 30 seconds.

◄ • ►

Variations

TROPICAL COCKTAIL Add ¼ cup coconut-flavored rum, 1 tablespoon banana liqueur, and ½ cup additional ice cubes before blending. Makes two 14-ounce drinks.

TROPICAL COCONUT SHAKE Substitute coconut ice cream or coconut sorbet for vanilla ice cream. Optional: add 4 tablespoons gold rum before blending.

TROPICAL PINEAPPLE SHAKE Substitute pineapple ice cream or pineapple sorbet for vanilla ice cream. Optional: add 4 tablespoons gold rum before blending.

VANILLA MALT

I F you don't like very sweet malts, use only 1 tablespoon of vanilla syrup and add ¼ teaspoon vanilla extract.

1½ cups ice cubes

3 scoops premium vanilla
   ice cream

1 cup milk

3 tablespoons malted milk
   powder

3 tablespoons vanilla syrup

Place all of the ingredients in a blender. Pulse the blender on and off until the mixture blends easily. Blend on high for 30 seconds or until smooth.

Variations

CHERRY VANILLA MALT Substitute cherry syrup for vanilla syrup. Add ¼ teaspoon vanilla extract. Proceed with the recipe as directed.

IRISH CREAM VANILLA MALT Add ¼ cup Irish cream liqueur before blending.

VANILLA BANANA MALT Add 1 small banana, sliced, before blending.

VANILLA COCONUT MALT Substitute unsweetened coconut milk for dairy milk.

VANILLA MAPLE MALT Substitute maple syrup for vanilla syrup.

VANILLA NUT MALT Substitute hazelnut or almond syrup for vanilla syrup and garnish with chopped toasted hazelnuts or almonds (see page xvi).

INDEX

ABOUT THE AUTHOR

Bruce Weinstein studied culinary arts at Johnson and Wales before opening a catering business in New York City. As a food consultant he has created recipes for Nabisco, Tropicana, House of Seagram, and Bols Liqueurs, among others. The author of *Frozen Drinks With or Without the Buzz,* he is a food writer and advertising executive who lives in Manhattan. He is currently writing a candy book for William Morrow.